T0209697

Bye-Bye Boobies

A cancer survivor's memoir
through grief, grace,
and celebration.

JOYCE VAN DYK

BALBOA.PRESS
A DIVISION OF HAY HOUSE

Copyright © 2023 Joyce Van Dyk.

All rights reserved. No part of this book may be used or reproduced by any means, graphic, electronic, or mechanical, including photocopying, recording, taping or by any information storage retrieval system without the written permission of the author except in the case of brief quotations embodied in critical articles and reviews.

This book is a work of non-fiction. Unless otherwise noted, the author and the publisher make no explicit guarantees as to the accuracy of the information contained in this book and in some cases, names of people and places have been altered to protect their privacy.

Balboa Press books may be ordered through booksellers or by contacting:

Balboa Press
A Division of Hay House
1663 Liberty Drive
Bloomington, IN 47403
www.balboapress.com
844-682-1282

Because of the dynamic nature of the Internet, any web addresses or links contained in this book may have changed since publication and may no longer be valid. The views expressed in this work are solely those of the author and do not necessarily reflect the views of the publisher, and the publisher hereby disclaims any responsibility for them.

The author of this book does not dispense medical advice or prescribe the use of any technique as a form of treatment for physical, emotional, or medical problems without the advice of a physician, either directly or indirectly. The intent of the author is only to offer information of a general nature to help you in your quest for emotional and spiritual well-being. In the event you use any of the information in this book for yourself, which is your constitutional right, the author and the publisher assume no responsibility for your actions.

Any people depicted in stock imagery provided by Getty Images are models, and such images are being used for illustrative purposes only.
Certain stock imagery © Getty Images.

Interior Image Credit: Rosabella Sinclair-Van Dyk

Print information available on the last page.

ISBN: 979-8-7652-4573-6 (sc)
ISBN: 979-8-7652-4572-9 (hc)
ISBN: 979-8-7652-4571-2 (e)

Library of Congress Control Number: 2023917941

Balboa Press rev. date: 01/27/2024

About This Book

On that crisp October morning, as I stood on the deck of my home, gazing out at the serene lake, I heard a voice within me that would forever change my life. The words were simple yet profound, "Your results are positive, but don't worry."

At that moment, I knew that the breast biopsy I had recently undergone would confirm what I already suspected - that I was embarking on my own journey of grief and healing.

My life has been shaped by experiences of grief and loss, including the loss of my brother during high school, my mother shortly after college, and my father in my early 30s. As a former pastor and hospital chaplain, I had also helped countless others navigate this path, but now it was my turn to face it head-on.

In Bye, Bye, Boobies, I share the story of my breast cancer journey—from mourning and grief to joy and celebration. This memoir offers a gift and guide to others whose lives are being invaded by breast cancer. It's also a resource for those who will have to make a decision to say goodbye to parts of a body that have served them well.

From throwing my own "Bye-Bye Boobies" party to discovering other creative and empowering ways to navigate cancer and grief, I hope this book provides useful tools, much-needed humor, and soulful guidance to help you on your own journey.

Joyce Van Dyk's humor, strong faith, honesty, and wisdom bring comfort and spiritual inspiration to those experiencing tests of faith.

-Rev. Marchiene Rienstra & Dr. John Rienstra, M.D.

Joyce Van Dyk vividly shares the challenges of her cancer diagnosis, which she faced with faith and determination. Her story is a beacon of hope for anyone confronting similar challenges.

-Rev. Lew Vander Meer, Sr. Pastor,
New Community Church, Grand Rapids, MI

Dedication

This book is dedicated to my dearly loved family. My beloved husband who has stood by my side through the good times and difficult times of my life. My beloved daughter, Kimberly Van Dyk and her husband Dr. Sam Cohen, and granddaughters Noelani and Rosabella Sinclair-Van Dyk. My dear son, Jeffery Van Dyk and his partner Pete Riherd. My awesome son Joshua Van Dyk and his dear wife Dr. Amanda Van Dyk and grandchildren Kaia and Levi Van Dyk.

Also, my siblings and their families. David and Jannelle Geertman, their children Tricia and Brian Schrotenboer, Kevin and Tara Geertman, Amy and John Ybarra. My sister Marilyn Chadderdon and her husband Pat, and children Ben, Marcus and Dr. Jackie Chadderdon. My sister Karen Geertman and her husband Ed, and children Brian Slizgi, Dr. Jason Slizgi, Kristen Slizgi and Francesco Marri.

A special thank you to dear friends, Dr. John Rienstra, Rev. Marchiene Rienstra, Rev. Lew Vander Meer, Dr. Mark Vander Meer, Rev. Jan Thorsen and the late Rev. Eric Thorsen, Joan Edson, Dr. Prudence Hall, Dr. Jim and Karen Visser, Dr. Russ and Dr. Karen Dempsey, Dr. Ariel Dempsey, Lee and Jean De Vries, the Sandusky family, Lori, Darrell, Paul, Kaela, Roth and Akeelah, Gary and Kathy Simmons, Judy Starr, Jane Johnson, Dr. Latayne C. Scott, Dr. Judi Childress, my cousins and many friends. Also, my dear friends Ardele Graham, Carol Jacobusse Hahnfeld, Sister Sue Tracy, Weldin and Mary Johnson, who have passed from this life to glory.

A special dedication to my beloved mother, Pearl Wierenga Geertman, my father, Marinus Geertman, my grandparents, Herman and Jennie Wierenga, Henry and Grace Geertman and my brother Jim Geertman all of whom I will see in heaven someday.

Thanksgiving and praise to our God for guidance and grace through this writing.

Acknowledgments Page

A special note of thanks to Rosabella Sinclair Van Dyk, Artist and granddaughter, for her artwork!

Spectrum Health
Lemmen Holton Cancer Center
Gilda's club
Dr. Karen and Russell Dempsey and Partners in Family Health Staff
Dr. Marianne Melnick, Kim Quigg PA, Surgical Oncology
Dr. Mark Campbell, Oncology Lemmen Holton Cancer Center
First Reformed Church, Holland Michigan
Dr. Latayne Scott, writer, researcher, Trinity Southwest University
Rev. Dr. Timothy Brown, President Emeritus Western Theological Seminary

Resource acknowledgment: Dr. Ronald Ramsey and Rene Noorbergen, Nikita Gill, Rev. Dr. Jacqui Lewis, C.S. Lewis, Fr Richard Rohr, Joyce Rupp OP, Dr. Henri Nouwen.

Contents

Introduction

For Everything There is a Season: Halloween Surprises and Falling Leaves

There is a time for everything,
and a season for every activity under the heavens:
a time to be born and a time to die,
a time to plant and a time to uproot,
a time to kill and a time to heal,
a time to tear down and a time to build,
a time to weep and a time to laugh,
a time to mourn and a time to dance,
a time to scatter stones and a time to gather them,
a time to embrace and a time to refrain from embracing,
a time to search and a time to give up,
a time to keep and a time to throw away,
a time to tear and a time to mend,
a time to be silent and a time to speak,
a time to love and a time to hate,
a time for war and a time for peace.

— Ecclesiastes 3:1-8.

Late October was my season to mourn but also to dance. It was a season to die and to be born again, it was a season of letting go of life and a season of regaining. It was a time to kill and a time to heal, a time to break down and a time to build up, a time to embrace all of life as if there was no tomorrow. It was a time of silence, a time to hate, a time to love, a time for war and a time for peace, it was the season of cancer.

It was also the season of surrender. October was here, the leaves had begun to shed. I remember picking up a leaf that was golden yellow, and the edges were already curled with brown. I ran my finger over the veins of the leaf, and I began to think of its history. Last spring it was a bud that, when nourished with the rain and sun, grew into a lovely sturdy leaf. I wondered how many leaves were on that tree? I wondered how many leaves this leaf had to say goodbye to before it fell.

As I held the leaf, I thought about how those leaves were being vulnerable enough to surrender and let go of their growth to the cold, harsh, unknown months of winter. Thus, they once again can grow their spring buds and begin their cycle of life. As I held the leaf in my hand, my thoughts drifted to the soon-to-be harsh winter months, I would be facing with Cancer. Somehow, I knew in the depths of my being, if I surrendered myself to whatever all the unknowns of this disease would be, I too could experience regrowth.

The "BIG C" had invaded my life. It has taken me several years to compile this story and the contents of what I call saying my goodbyes, a book for healing. This book is intended to be a gift and guide to help my sisters worldwide whose lives are being invaded by breast cancer. It is also a resource for those who will have to make a decision, which requires us to say goodbye to parts of our bodies that have served us well. It is meant to be an aid to anyone who is facing the loss of any body part.

We are fearfully and wonderfully made human beings and whether we are losing our breasts, a limb, an eye, a kidney or an organ, receiving this type of news is jolting, sobering and it is a time for mourning. On the flip side of life, it is also a time to be thankful for the many ways your body part has served you in life.

This book includes many of the insights I gained through my cancer journeys and creative ways to cope with loss. I have found one of the ways to cope with loss is to allow mourning or grief to hold its rightful position. For me, it was important to allow time to grieve, in order to move forward to a position of gratitude and thanks for the many ways my body parts served me well. It was a time to be thankful for the role the teacher of cancer could provide in my life.

But you may say, I didn't invite or ask for cancer, or any other disease you are dealing with. But didn't you? In some fashion or way, I believe we are all given difficult situations in life to teach us life lessons and to hone us into the person we still need to be. Remember, the school of life involves pain, loss and death, part of the human experience, so when cancer is diagnosed, often people find themselves asking "Why me?" Perhaps they blame themselves for not taking care of their body as they should have, or ask the question: Why is God punishing me?

Perhaps a better solution to these questions is "Why not me?" While seeking answers to questions such as: What can I learn from this experience? How can I grow, while looking for the meaning of this disease in my life? You may find yourself questioning things you never thought of before. This journey through cancer can be extremely valuable in finding the true meaning of life and finding God in your time of trouble. What a gift that is! If you have spiritual questions, search your soul for answers and perhaps a pastor or counselor who can help you work through these areas of life.

Cancer certainly has its ups and downs in life, good days, bad days, days when you are overwhelmed with stress, and days when you are confident that you can beat this disease. On good days, go for a cup of coffee with a friend and just enjoy the good day. On bad days remind yourself it's okay to have a bad day and that tomorrow may be better and brighter. Take one day at a time, take care of yourself the best you can, and you will probably find the intensity of your emotions begin to lessen as you surrender to your disease and allow yourself to grow through it.

If you are a student of life and seek to grow and learn from this experience, then you can make it your intention to move forward to the next phases of life no matter how difficult it may be. I have found that as we develop firm intentions to learn from the school of life, we also will allow grace and God to walk with us during this time of shedding leaves into a beautiful full blooming tree reaching its branches towards the heavens again.

Friend, are you ready to take a leap of faith, armed with trembling courage to fight the cancer journey? As you receive this news, I pray you will be able to move ahead step by step and find the inner courage that you thought you never had. Your story is just beginning as you discover the courage and strength to fight this disease. Always, remember you can do this — you are strong! Take heart in Philippians 4:13: "I can do all things through Christ who strengthens me."

Remember, fear cannot control you, but feeding it with our doubts and worries can. Fear can turn your life into a tornado of destructive thoughts if you let it. The best thing you can do when destructive thoughts enter your mind is to replace them with faith. Faith in God to see you through. Faith in yourself to move forward with courage. Faith in your medical team to bring about the best possible results for you. Do not let fear control you, instead choose courage! Recite and remember the words from 2 Timothy 1:7: "For the Spirit God gave us does not make us timid, but gives us power, love and self-discipline."

So, choose courage!

We've all heard the phrase, "When life gives you lemons, make lemonade". Sometimes life is not fair and it is a hard pill to swallow. In the midst of tough times be strong, be brave, be an overcomer. Even in our lowest of times when the lemons are most sour, there is always a glimmer of hope just waiting to write a new story for your life. It may be like finding a needle in a haystack but it is there — that glimmer of hope. Just reach out and grab that glimmer and hang on to it with all you have. With hope and faith on your side, miracles can happen and sometimes life gives you a second chance. Hold on, own it and move forward and the lemonade will refresh you.

Have you ever met a strong person who has not had adverse times? Maybe this time in your life of trials you are developing strengths in yourself you did not know you had. So, on bad days, refuse to stay down, get up, refuse to give in or throw in the towel. Look your day in the eye and smile! You are so much stronger than you think; and remember as long as you are alive there is hope.

Remember and recite the words from Jeremiah 29:11.

> "'For I know the plans I have for you," declares the Lord, "plans to prosper you and not to harm you, plans to give you hope and a future.'"

PART ONE

MY PATHWAY THROUGH CANCER

BREATHE

Breathe on me Breath of Life,
Breathe on me Giver of Life,
Breathe into me the dawn of a new day,
Breathe Life, Breathe Wellness, Breathe Renewal.
Breathe Hope and Infinite Possibilities
Breathe peace into my fragmented soul,
Breathe warmth to my weary bones
And calm to my spirit,
Renew my cells and heal this body, I pray.

My body warms now with peace,
For God is here, He is with me,
He walks with me in my tears,
And takes away my fears.
He wraps me in His gentle blanket of love,
Great God of warmth,
My trust is in you, O Radiant One,
I melt into your goodness,
As I yield to you and all is well.

—Joyce Van Dyk

CHAPTER ONE

The Diagnosis

So do not fear, for I am with you;
do not be dismayed, for I am your God.
I will strengthen you and help you;
I will uphold you with my righteous right hand.
—(Isaiah 41:10

I'LL NEVER FORGET THE SCENE. MY FRIEND AND PHYSICIAN DR. KAREN came into her office where I was seated, awaiting news. At first, she tried to make some small talk as she thumbed through my test results.

"Dr. Karen," I said, "I already know the results of my biopsy are positive, I just need to know what to do." Her eyes filled first with surprise, and then with tears.

"How did you know?" she asked. I told her what had happened in the last few days.

I had a biopsy procedure on Friday and spent hours wondering about the "what ifs" of cancer and trying to proceed as normal. The next day, Halloween Oct. 31, I was awakened to the last of an Indian summer. The sun was shining against a deep blue sky where rays of color seemed to smear across the horizon at the opening of the day. The billowy clouds seemed to take on forms of mountain peaks.

As I stood on our deck overlooking the lake we lived on, the sun warmed my body as its rays shone on the water, which seemed to be dancing like sparkling diamonds. It indeed was the perfect setting for a fall day, with the golden hues of autumn trees ablaze with color. I stood there amazed at the beauty of creation.

As I stood in silence, I sensed an inner voice saying, "Your test results are positive."

At that moment peace engulfed my body like gentle waves upon the seashore, as the sun warmed my spirit and soul.

By 4:00 in the afternoon a sudden shift in the weather occurred, the winds picked up, the clouds turned black and a storm set in. I thought, just as surely as the sun shines and peace is prevalent, so too there will be the dark stormy days ahead.

Yet, it was well with my soul.

JOYCE'S SONG

All will be well, all will be well.
All will be well, don't worry.
Take courage, be strong,
All will be well.

Verse 1
I remember the day so clearly,
The golden sun falling on the lake, sparkling like diamonds.
I felt an overwhelming peace that everything was going to be ok,
But my Cancer was positive.
And then I heard a voice inside me saying, "All will be well."

All will be well, all will be well,
All will be well, don't you worry.
Take courage, be strong,
All will be well.

Verse 2
At times, depression and all the decisions overwhelm me,
As I deal with these feelings of
losing my breasts, my female identity, the surgeries, the reconstruction, the pain, the chemo, the radiation, and the days and months and years ahead made my head swirl.
Then I recall the cross of suffering, remembering that the big "C" in Christ is stronger than the little "c" of cancer. And I know,

All will be well, all will be well,
All will be well, don't you worry.
Take courage, be strong,
All will be well.

Verse 3
How do you find some kind of closure?
To lose a part of your body that has served you well?

How do you find alternative ways to keep your attitude in check, so that the days ahead are filled with healing grace and peace?
I knew my attitude would be the painting, which would color my world, so I knew I wanted to include my friends in painting the canvas of this journey I was taking.

All will be well, all will be well.
All will be well, don't you worry.
Take courage, be strong,
All will be well.

—Joyce Van Dyk

CHAPTER TWO

When Sorrow Ambushes You

Not only so, but we also glory in our sufferings, because we know that suffering produces perseverance; perseverance, character; and character, hope.

— Romans 5:3-4

I knew all would be well, because I knew how God had brought me through difficult circumstances before.

I thought back to another beautiful day, this one decades before on a spring day in early April. Tree buds had just produced their tender almost lime green leaves in Michigan. Some of the leaves looked so delicate with a lacy effect, the veins so distinct that they mapped out their various shapes. The skies had turned from winter grays to hues of blues with white billowy cloud formations opening towards the heavens and welcoming spring. It was the kind of day when a spring jacket would be due and the air I breathed was as fresh as orange sherbet on a hot day, cool and refreshing.

I will never forget the sight of my 16-year-old brother, Jim, riding his shiny black Schwinn bike down the street with a red beginner's two-wheel bike strapped to his shoulders. Mom had told our family to wait outside because Jim was to come home with a surprise. There we stood in the front yard watching him pedal down our street with a broad smile, and the twinkle in his bright blue eyes was a sign of pure joy! When he reached our house, he got off his bike and unstrapped the shiny red bike from his back. He knelt down and looked at my five-year-old sister Karen.

"Little sister, this bike is for you!"

"For me?" Karen was wide-eyed, jumping up and down.

Jim picked up Karen and put her on the bike seat and ran alongside her, balancing the bike as she squealed for joy. He did this every day for a week until she gained confidence and was able to balance on her own.

At that time, Jim had a part-time job at a photography shop after school and had saved up money from his paychecks for this bike for our sister. The owner of Reliable Cycle Bike Shop, Mr. Ken, was a friend from church and gave Jim a good deal as they always did for their friends. I have no idea how long he had saved his money for this bike, but the memory of that kind act has always stayed with us.

Earlier that year, Jim had become an Eagle Scout and was always involved in doing kind deeds for others. The Sunday after Karen had received her bike Jim said he wanted to take our family portrait with his new camera. After church, he set up his camera for the family portrait.

He put his camera on a tripod and set a timer and jumped into the picture as the camera clicked away. There we were, all five children and mom and dad for our first family portrait!

The following week after dinner we had our normal family devotions. Since there were seven of us in the family, we each were assigned one day of the week to do devotions, with mom helping the younger ones. That evening, it was Jim's turn. He chose to read from the book of Job in the Bible. Job, as you may recall, had many trials and struggles including losing his entire family.

Jim ended his reading and said, "What would we do if we had to lose a member of our family? How would we feel? Would we be mad at God?"

There was silence among us.

"It's food for thought," I said, "But we are all healthy, why would God take one of us?" As a 17-year-old sister, I thought certainly we had too much to live for —to think of a possible death of any of us was just too much.

After dinner, I cleared the table and began to do the dishes and those thoughts lingered through my mind. Jim went down in the basement, where he had his photography equipment, to arrange photos for his journalism class as he was one of the school's photographers/journalists for our Holland High School paper.

The following morning Jim awoke and did not feel well. He insisted on going to school to bring his photos and articles to the journalism room. At that time my mother worked in the high school counseling office and after Jim returned from the journalism room, he headed to mom's office saying he felt really sick. He had a horrible headache and felt sick to his stomach.

Mom had him lie down in the first aid room next to her office and gave him some aspirin. He was running a temperature and mom sat with him thinking she should drive him home, when he began going into convulsions and choking on his vomit. The counselor next to her office came in and began CPR, while mom called the ambulance.

My mom called Dykstra Funeral and Ambulance service, members of our local church and friends of my parents. Soon the ambulance was at school taking Jim, my mom and Mrs. Eddie the counselor to the hospital, which was a short two miles from the high school. When they got to the hospital Jim was rushed to emergency where they did an emergency tracheotomy with no success and Jim was pronounced dead.

The next thing I knew, I was pulled out of my first hour class and rushed home by another counselor, Mr. C, to wake my dad up, who at that time was working third shift. I told Dad to rush and put on his clothes because Jim was seriously sick in the hospital. Dad threw on his clothes and met me outside where an ambulance was waiting to take us to the hospital. When we arrived at the hospital emergency room we were escorted to a small room where my mom was crying and the doctor told us that Jim had expired!

"Dead, you mean?" I said. "No! No! No!"

I began weeping uncontrollably along with Mom and Dad. I sat in shock and shaking and full of emotions.as Mrs. Eddie held me. No, I thought this could not be happening to a young, healthy 16-year-old boy! Dead! No! It felt like every bit of our flesh had been ripped open by this news!

That day became a blur, but our family discussion of the story of Job came to mind over and over again. Was this all a premonition of death that Jim had? What about the bike for Karen and the family portrait that Jim wanted to take? What did he know that he did not tell us?

Oh my God, how could you possibly take Jim, a young man with so much potential? Our neighbor, Mr. Marv, went to the elementary school to get our other siblings Dave, Marilyn and Karen. When they got home Mom and Dad told them that Jim had died. I remember in particular Dave crumbling to the ground in tears. He and Jim shared a bedroom and he looked up to his older brother with such fondness; and Marilyn in third grade and Karen in kindergarten, none really could comprehend.

The next day our family went to the funeral home to find a casket and prepare for Jim's funeral. It was all so surreal. It felt like we were just going through the motions and not much was registering. The lumps in our throats were so large we could barely swallow and every time the funeral director, our family friend, Mr. K., asked a question, we would be in tears, tears of shock and denial and he would be wiping tears from his eyes too. I can't help but think how difficult it was for them to prepare Jim's body for viewing because of family ties.

As Jim laid in that casket, he looked so normal, like a healthy teenager. Friends and family poured into the funeral home to express their sympathy. The line of people seemed to be endless, but for me it was so very hard to greet our mutual classmates, who were saying their goodbyes to a well-liked friend. That year took the lives of other Holland area classmates who had been killed in an automobile accident and another classmate committed suicide. Jim made number five.

He died on April 19, one of the longest and saddest days in my life. That week felt like a blur. Not much registered, except the gnawing pain that felt as if it would never go away. It was not just my pain, but watching all of my family in pain felt debilitating. One of us would begin crying and it set off the rest of us in tears, and then to see your classmates in tears shattered my heart. I was so glad for their support, but none of us was yet acquainted with grief until these deaths hit our school. Jim's death consumed our families' thoughts and I felt guilty for every sibling fight we ever had. I assume my dad felt guilty too, as he sometimes lost his temper with me, Jim and Dave.

Where was God in all of this? What were we to do without Jim? My mom was literally torn apart, shattered and broken.

Our pastor from First Reformed Church immediately reached out to us, listened with a great deal of empathy, as he too had lost a son. The day of Jim's funeral the school was closed for teachers and students to attend the funeral. The church was packed and overflowing. I remember our pastor's message to a church full of grieving people as one of love and compassion of honoring my brother. Much of his message to this day is a blur, but his love and compassion was very sincere and comforting. In many ways, our pastor represented God with skin on and a heart of love.

As Jim's 17- year-old sister, I sat beside the gravesite wondering where God was in the midst of Jim's death. There was something in me that vehemently opposed laying my brother in the ground and throwing dirt on that casket. It felt so final. I felt numb and angry and I wanted to scream out in anger and protest that this death had even happened! It felt like my heart had been ripped open in pain.

Suddenly a dove came swooping by, perching itself in front of me and then flying off to the heavens. In that moment a peace came over me, knowing my brother was in heaven, with Jesus.

Were my questions answered as to why God would allow a young vibrant 16-year-old boy to die from choking on his vomit? No. Did I wrestle with questions? Yes. But in that moment as the dove flew off into the heavens, I sensed a great amount of peace and grace touched my grieving heart, and I knew God's plans for Jim were greater than my parents' dreams for him. And every time I questioned God, the memory of the dove came to mind and peace filled my heart, until I could leave my brother in God's safe hands. God has often sent me doves and butterflies as a sign that He is with me. Even in the midst of deep grief I could sense His presence through the sign of a dove.

I still have a pair of doves that visit my deck every spring and it always brings me peace and gives me hope. What signs has God sent your way?

JIM'S CLIMB

He was a runner for life,
An energetic young man of 16.
Searching and digging into life,
As if there would be no tomorrow.

So full of life, love and fun,
In search of the good and beautiful.
In search of the whys of life,
In search of the truth.

His broad smile and laughter,
Greeted each day,
Along with his boyish
Mischievous ways.

Jim was abundant in giving,
And doing good deeds,
A number one Boy Scout
Was he!

He used his first paycheck
To buy his little sister Karen a bike,
And rescued pigeons with his younger brother Dave,
Nursing them to health, until they could fly.

He was lover of nature, good fun and life,
Now we sit at his gravesite,
Asking why?
Why death, why he?

A son of Bub and Pearl,
A brother to Joyce, Dave, Marilyn and Karen,
A cousin, a friend to many,
A young life snatched from all of its potential.

Why death, God, why he?
Is death a demonic thief?
At the gravesite we stand,
Numbed to think of our grief and loss.

While standing in silence,
A dove soared gracefully by the gravesite
and then soared to the heavens
And seemed to say,
You may not understand,
But all is ok. All is ok.

—Joyce Van Dyk, age 17

CHAPTER THREE

My Cancer Journey Begins

And my God will meet all your needs according to the riches of his glory in Christ Jesus.

— Philippians 4:19

As a woman with a family history of cancer, I was religious about getting mammograms. My mother, Pearl Wierenga Geertman, passed away at age 50 from metastatic breast cancer. Mom was first diagnosed at age 40 and had a mastectomy, chemo and radiation. There was a ten-year period between her initial diagnosis and her death on June 19.

During those years there were times her cancer was at bay, and other times it reared its ugly head. Cancer never gave us a warning as to when it would metastasize to another area of her body. Cancer was like a teeter totter, up and down, taking more of mom each time it recurred. We lived between surgeries, chemo, radiation, remission and recurrence, not knowing whether the reports would come back positive or negative. Living with mom's cancer was like living on the edge of a cliff, trying to seek balance, but never sure of going over the cliff.

My mother's father, my grandfather, Herman Wierenga, also passed away at age 59 from cancer, as well as my aunt Lois on my mom's side. Also, cancer took the life of my Uncle Ted and a cousin on my dad's side. Cancer had become a family word we all feared.

The year of my own diagnosis I found myself getting physically very tired at work. I had been on the pastoral staff of churches for the last 15 years, and while I really loved my work and the people, my energy level was decreasing and I was debating about resigning and taking a rest, shifting gears, taking my Clinical Pastoral courses and do some part-time chaplaincy work at our local hospital in Grand Rapids, Michigan, where I had done volunteer chaplaincy work for many years.

Many days in the month of October as I would leave work at the hospital, I would drive by the Betty Ford Women's Breast Cancer Clinic. Something in my mind would say, go get a mammogram and do it now. Like most people, I kind of dismissed the thought and rationalized that it was not yet time for a scheduled mammogram. However, after the third time passing by the Betty Ford Breast Clinic and being prompted to call for a mammogram, I thought maybe I should pay attention to this voice that was speaking to me.

I got home and called for an appointment, thinking that they would probably say for insurance reasons I would have to wait until after January for a scheduled mammogram. However, as divine appointment would have it, they told me I was scheduled for mammograms every 6 months because of my family history, which I was unaware of. There was an opening that Thursday evening, which we scheduled.

The mammogram went as mammograms usually do… squish, squash, smash! Since the radiologist was not on duty until morning to read the results, I went on my way. The next morning, they called me and said something suspicious showed up on the mammogram and would I please come back in for more testing that day. It was 8:00 am and they had an opening for 11:00 that morning.

I saw the radiologist, who repeated the mammogram, did an ultrasound, and said they would like to do a needle biopsy of the area. I hated needles and thought they'd schedule an appointment for the following week, but the radiology oncologist said he wanted to proceed with it immediately.

I called my husband at work and told him what they were going to do and that I would see him for dinner. Lucky for me, I did not have time to think about it. The procedure went smoothly, without too much pain and it was fun watching them remove spaghetti-like tissues.

The morning after my biopsy procedure my dear friend and family physician Dr. Karen called and asked me if I would like my biopsy results before Wednesday, November 3, which was my annual physical appointment. She said she would be getting the biopsy results on Monday, November 1.

"Thank you," I said, "I can wait until November 3, which is also my birthday." Many people said oh my, what news to get on your birthday. In retrospect, that news was my birthday gift, because it gave me the opportunity to get things in order for this journey.

On the morning of November 3, Dr. Karen read to me my diagnosis. I remember, hearing her words, trying to take in all she was saying and yet feeling a sense of inner peace.

Karen is an exceptionally caring physician and went on to tell me the results and the type of cancer I had. She recommended a bilateral mastectomy along with chemo and asked what surgeon I wanted. I didn't even have to think twice about that and knew I wanted another dear friend and physician, Dr. John, for my surgery. That night I called Dr. John at home and told him of the test results.

"Joyce, meet me in my office tomorrow at 11:00 a.m.," he said, "and bring your husband and daughter along."

After Dr. John's examination and review of the reports he said, "Even though I did your hysterectomy 10 years ago when you had the early stages of an ovarian tumor, I feel you are too much like a sister, and I just cannot ethically do your surgery. I want to refer you to my friend, who did my wife's breast cancer surgery. I want to make sure you have the same treatment as my wife, Marchiene or (Marty)."

For me, that was so reassuring, because John's wife Marty is such a wonderful human being and has been a dear friend and mentor to me for years. She is a minister and was one of my professors at Western Theological Seminary in Holland, Michigan. Again, I thought it would probably take a week for me to get to see that doctor, but Dr. John called him, and he met me during his lunch hour the next day. Definitely, everything was working in divine order!

Dr. D. turned out to be the marvelous caring human being that John had described. After the examination and review of my case, Dr. D. told me of his wife's breast cancer, gave me their home phone number, and said if I wanted to talk to another woman, to give her a call.

Just imagine the inner peace and direction I was beginning to feel as each doctor took me under their wings. Actually, throughout this whole personal journey, God showed me the heart of each physician who cared for me. In today's world, we often hear negative comments about doctors and hospitals, comments about what they should have done and didn't do. But for me, I felt like one lucky and blessed person each time I had to talk to another professional. I had doctors that I knew were personally on my side, as well as those I had never met and each one answered my questions and met my needs with dignity. How important it is to treat a woman with dignity, even more so, when she is about to lose her breasts.

Before scheduling the surgery, the doctor set me up with a team of surgeons to discuss my case. I met with oncologists, plastic surgeons, geneticists, radiologists, etc. After all tests were in, their best opinion for me was a bilateral mastectomy followed by chemotherapy.

I'll have to admit, one of the biggest hurdles to overcome in the preparation time before surgery was dealing with so many doctors prodding my breasts, taking measurements and pictures of my breasts. At one time, during a photo shoot, the camera failed, and the intern that was taking the pictures seemed to take eons to figure out the problem, while I stood naked from the waist up!

Well, let me tell you, having doctors photograph your breasts in so many different positions is a journey in itself! What a Kodak moment!

CHAPTER FOUR

A Heritage of Cancer

He will wipe every tear from their eyes. There will be no more death or mourning or crying or pain, for the old order of things has passed away.

— Revelation 21:4

JUST AS I CARRIED IN MY HEART FOR DECADES THE QUESTIONS AND sorrows associated with my brother's sudden death, I also carried another burden – knowing the path that cancer had taken in my mother's life.

About five years after my brother Jim's death, my mother's cancer recurred. Mom went through many surgeries and treatments as cancer swept through her body. She fought the good fight with faith but eventually succumbed to cancer.

My mom, Pearl Lillian Wierenga Geertman, was a shining light in this world. She had a wonderful, compassionate, gentle spirit with a friendly smile that was magnetic. Unlike me, she was tall with a slim build and brown hair. I have more of my dad's looks, blonde, average height and always having to watch my weight. My mom's personality I share. Both mom and dad had lots of friends and I remember with fondness many activities with other families.

Unfortunately, as I was growing up, my dad's growing use of alcohol darkened our days. He used alcohol as a negative coping mechanism and it carried over into his family and business life. My dad had his good days when life was great, but when things got tough, drinking became the enemy from which we would run!

We lived with a father who was an elder in the church and whose behavior and temper when compounded with alcohol was very frightening. There were days we did not know which dad we would have to deal with or run from. I remember many times that my mom and I would hunt down his hidden whiskey bottles and dump them down the kitchen drain.

When Mom got sick, alcohol became more of a coping mechanism for dad's sad spirit. Losing mom was more than he could deal with and the Veterans of Foreign War post was often where he hung out to drink with his buddies and he would come home in the wee hours of the morning.

On the other side of my family, my mom and Grandpa and Grandma Wierenga were always active in their church and community, serving on the school board and as elected officials with many civic duties. We were raised by our mom and grandpa and grandma to be active in our greater community and church, to bloom where we were planted. I was grateful for that heritage.

When mom's cancer recurred, it had spread throughout her body, to the bones, lungs, brain. She had been in and out of the hospital for surgeries, chemo and radiation for nearly a year. During her last week of life, Mom had been in a coma and when she awoke and regained consciousness, she began telling us that she had just seen Jesus. She went on to say that heaven was so very beautiful, that she saw colors and flowers she had never seen before, and that the heavenly music was an angelic thousand voice choir and so beautiful!

"I saw your brother and grandpa" mom told us, "And Jim and Grandpa Wierenga were so happy! I just want to be able to see each of you there someday."

The four of us siblings ages 11, 14, 18, and myself age 22 sat around her bed, as she fed us our last meal. It was a spiritual meal, our last supper. The meal consisted of story-telling, words of wisdom, grace, compassion, and faith lessons imparted from Mom with deep love. She talked to each child, telling them of her love for them and shared her deepest wishes and direction for our lives. as she hugged and kissed us. I was the last child she talked with.

Joyce, she said to me, "you are the oldest, and I want you to watch over your siblings." She then told me what each one would need to carry on through this difficult time.

"Some will feel afraid and will go their own way, but they will come back. Pray for them, be there for them, keep the family together.

"I love you all so very much," she said, her voice weakening, "and someday, we will all be together in heaven."

This was our last supper filled with love and kisses for dessert. Needless to say, we were all filled with tears. In retrospect, her dying words were her most life-giving words.

When our brother died, we could not make much sense of it. This time was different: much grief and tears, yes, but in mom's dying she planted seeds of life and hope that have carried us through life.

Mom died the next day on June 19 at the age of 50. You see, my mom Pearl Lillian Wierenga Geertman lived with praise and love, grief and life side by side. Mom's parting words were her greatest gift to us! I hope to leave this world as mom did with praise on my lips and love in my heart as I too, will say my goodbyes to my loved ones some-day.

Everyday life lets us see how short life can be, so it is important to always leave your loved ones knowing how special they are to you. Through death experiences and cancer, I have come to embrace the preciousness and fragility of life. We take so much for granted until it is not there. Why does it take catastrophes to connect with each other in a meaningful way? Even if conversations of depth are uncomfortable, why not practice uncovering some of those layers now, before it's too late. If this is hard for you, consider asking a pastor or counselor for help.

Two days after mom's funeral my husband, Dick, was drafted into the Army and left for basic training. So, I moved back home to help my father and siblings for the rest of that year. When Dick finished basic training, he was sent to Picatinny Arsenal in Dover, New Jersey where he was assigned to work on arsenal logic controls. I had our baby daughter, Kimberly Pearl during that time and was allowed to join him in off base housing when Kimberly was 3 months old.

My siblings and I experienced what it is to be motherless, the loneliness that follows death, where there is no longer a sense of belonging. Mom was always the one who held our family together and without her we felt lost. On the other hand, as siblings we hung onto each other for support. The bond my siblings and I formed through this time will last until the day we die. We have always been with each other through thick and thin. My children, as well as our nieces and nephews, have witnessed this bond and have formed a deep love for each other.

I may never understand the whys of these early deaths, but I did experience the grace of God and a peace that passes understanding. I remain grateful that we have a close family because we have shared in each other's joys and sorrows. Thank you, family.

I have since gained glimpses of God's plan and while I will always miss Mom, I have been able to leave her in God's good care. But when I reach heaven, I'll have lots of questions for God.

On the other hand, once I reach heaven perhaps none of my questions will be important, as I will be walking a heavenly walk!

CHAPTER FIVE

Attitudes and Beatitudes and Thanksgiving Living

You restored me to health and let me live. Surely it was for my benefit that I suffered such anguish. In your love you kept me from the pit of destruction; you have put all my sins behind your back.

— Isaiah 38:16-17

ONE OF THE MOST UNCOMFORTABLE ASPECTS OF HEALING FROM surgery is wondering how your spouse or partner will deal with your body changes. I found that the sooner they can help with your care, the more comfortable you will become and the more they will empathize with your loss and theirs too. For some people, just looking at blood is difficult. Luckily, for me, my husband has always had a strong stomach so he would help with emptying the drain tubes and bandaging me. When Dick was at work, often one of my children would help me with these tasks and after about two weeks of healing the draining stopped and I could have the tubes removed. I loved the way my family helped me with such dignity and pure love!

One thing I noticed while going through breast cancer was how uncomfortable even women are when talking about breasts or other intimate body parts that are damaged, partly because it is intimate. Oh yes, people can talk dirty about breasts with their jokes, but when it becomes personal, it's a different story.

I thought, "Oh Lord, you created all of me, my arms, legs, nose, and if any of those parts were injured nobody would be reluctant to talk about it." People would often be quick to ask how I was doing and quickly change the subject, because they were uncomfortable talking about my illness. Even when I might respond, "I am doing fairly well, but this week has been rough," some would quickly shy away and change the subject.

In retrospect, this would be a perfect time to lend a listening ear. Now, I might be a bit more sensitive to this, because my life and profession required a listening and compassionate ear and this is not always natural for people, but it can be developed. I knew that all my Creator endowed me with was fearfully and wonderfully made. To ignore talking about difficulties, in a time of need, seemed to be ignoring the fact of who we are as people.

That is precisely why I find it important to find ways where we as women can gather to share and celebrate the beautiful and creative ways we are gifted and give voice to that which is within us. In doing so, we also provide a way for all women to have their voice heard and to celebrate all that we have been endowed or gifted with. Too often in our patriarchal society, women's voices have been ignored in the church, community, government etc. It is getting better, but we have a long way to go to have our voices heard.

I must admit, in my experience with breast cancer the first time around, it was always male physicians advising me what to do and I felt somewhat intimated. While I know they were approaching my disease from a medical perspective, I do feel there were times when we both would have benefited from listening to each other. For a male doctor, listening to the voice of their female patient is very important.

During my second breast cancer diagnosis I purposely chose to have a woman oncologist Dr. M. and her PA Kim. I felt more comfortable and felt like I was heard and affirmed.

As with most significant journeys in life, I was not meant to take my cancer journey alone. My good husband, Dick, as well as my dear children, Kimberly, Dr. Sam, Jeffery, Pete Joshua, and Dr. Amanda, grandchildren Noelani and Rosabell, Kaia and Levi played a significant role on my cancer journeys. How thankful I was for their love and support. They were my heroes!

Many questions entered my mind during this phase: How would I feel about my womanhood and sexuality after losing my breasts? How would my reconstructed breasts look? How would my husband feel about our sexuality together? Would he ever see me again as a whole and complete woman? Would I ever again see myself as a whole woman?

Fortunately, a few of my doctors who had gone through this journey with their wives became wonderful role models for my husband. They would often talk to him about the surgeries and what to expect, as well as conversations about the attitudes of a husband towards his wife after breast cancer surgery. Both Dick and I were about to find out what our human sexuality was really about. We were about to find that the true extension of our love ran far deeper than any sexual journey we could possibly take.

I went to a medical library and studied what was involved in a bilateral mastectomy. I knew my post-surgery image would look distorted and began looking for ways I could find positive images to focus on prior to surgery. I began posting positive image statements on my bathroom mirror and seeing myself as beautiful, regardless of what was being taken from me. I began to thank God for the life he gave me during my pre-cancer years, as a loving wife to my husband and a nurturing mother.

I looked at many pictures of breast reconstruction and prayed for the ability to one day see myself as whole. Yes, this journey was not only filled with deep physical pain, but it was also about discovering the deep fires I was about to enter.

This cancer journey was about discovering the wholeness one can experience while going through the fire, and allowing those flames to go up and burn until pureness is formed and beauty forms a new image of wholeness in me.

Yes, I was about to find the golden nugget, of who I am as a woman and who we are as a committed couple.

SPECIAL SECTION:

QUESTIONS TO ASK YOUR HEALTH PROVIDER ABOUT YOUR CANCER DIAGNOSIS

Spectrum Health (now Corewell Health) gives their cancer patients a list of questions to ask about any Cancer disease and treatment. As an active member of your health care team, you have the right to ask questions about your Cancer and treatments. Spectrum Health's book gives a list of questions to ask your physicians and suggests you take notes.

A sample of questions to ask are as follows:

* What kind of cancer do I have? Is it invasive?
* What lab tests were completed and what did they show?
* Do I need any additional lab tests or diagnostic studies?
* What is the purpose of each study or test?
* How will this information help decide what types of further tests or treatments I should have?
* Could there be an inherited component to my disease? If so, should I pursue genetic testing?
* What are my treatment choices?
* Will I have to be in the hospital and for how long?
* Are there any new treatments or clinical trials that I should consider?
* How will we know if this is working?
* How will each treatment affect my daily life?
* What are the chances of the cancer coming back again?
* What is the goal of my treatment?

CHAPTER SIX

Throw a Party!

A cheerful heart is good medicine, but a crushed spirit dries up the bones.

— Proverbs 17:22

A few of the wonderful gifts God has blessed me with is the ability to be transparent, have fun and enjoy humor even when things are tough. I began to feel the need to do something fun, before my surgery, which would allow me to laugh and not take life too seriously while on this journey.

For me, this included a gathering where I could laugh and share with my friends and family. A place where we could embrace the joys and gifts of womanhood that provided nurture, love, and comfort. A place where I could laugh and smile.

Fortunately, God blessed me with the joy of a wonderful chaplain colleague and mentor on this journey. Can you believe, a Franciscan nun, whose sense of humor took her on speaking tours as a multiple cancer survivor? Yes, Sister Sue in the flesh, was the one God not only dropped in my lap to laugh and pray with me through this journey, but she was my mentor in the Chaplaincy program at Spectrum Hospital.

On a regular basis we would meet, not only to discuss the patient load I was carrying at the hospital, but also to discuss how I was personally dealing with my own illness in relation to the patients I would see. Somehow, our conversations would always have some humor inserted and I knew that this humor and laughter would serve me well through this journey.

I remember saying to Sister Sue, "I need to find a way to share this journey with friends who would laugh and cry with me." instantly, I came up with the idea of having a "Bye, Bye Boobie Party"! Just the thought of it made us both laugh, and I was on a roll to have some fun before the surgery.

I immediately went over to my daughter Kimberly's house and shared with her the idea of having this Bye, Bye Boobie Party. She thought it was great and was willing to host it. The next several days I spent much time thinking about the type of party I wanted... but one thing I knew for sure was that I did not want the party at my house, mainly because I didn't want the pressure of cleaning my house for the event!

Kimberly asked my neighbors, Weldin and Jane Johnson, if we could have the party at their home. "Yes! Of course!" was the answer. And we were on a roll!

I was now on my way to the next adventures of party planning! Since I had never done such a party or heard of anyone else who had... I wanted it to be fun and healing for me and my guests.

The subject of healing for me has come to encompass the physical, emotional, and spiritual journey that one must go through, to experience wholeness as a person with an illness. As a pastor and chaplain, I had visited countless people with many types of illness and had come to appreciate and believe in the interdisciplinary roles of healing for the whole person. I knew well the power of prayer in healing. I also knew how deeply one needed to connect with family and friends. I knew well the need for modern medicine, research, and good physicians. I had excellent physicians and knew the best of research and medicine would soon be part of my life.

But what I still needed was that special group of friends who could gather with me, and with whom I could be transparent on my cancer journey. I needed those who could pray for me, those who could cry with me, and those who could just let me talk and laugh, through this major pre-surgery time of life.

I knew I wanted on my guest list about a dozen good supporters to gather with me before this surgery. I decided they could not be family members, simply because cancer has been an emotional roller coaster in my family affecting generations back as far as I could remember. Instinctively, I knew that this event would be too emotional for my family members and me. I made my list which consisted of friends I had grown to trust and love, friends I had journeyed through life with and had shared in many of their trials. They were friends I could be my funny self with and yet be serious. Yep, my list was made… a dozen amazing women I would invite!

CHAPTER SEVEN

Party Preparations and Instructions

Heal me, Lord, and I will be healed;
save me and I will be saved,
for you are the one I praise.
—Jeremiah 17:14

I ASKED MY DAUGHTER, KIMBERLY, TO MAKE UP THE INVITATIONS FOR a Bye, Bye Boobie Party to be held on the weekend just before my surgery on Monday. The invitation had drawn beautiful breasts, as shown in this picture.

You are invited to a

For: Joyce Van Dyk
Date: November 30
Time: 3:00 pm
Location: Joyce's home
What to bring: A story of how you know Joyce, plus a poem, song, reading, etc. about breasts. Be funny or serious - just be creative and bring something to encourage her on her breast cancer journey.
RSVP to: Her daughter, Kimberly

On the party invitation was written: "You are invited to a Bye, Bye, Boobie Party for Joyce Van Dyk."

Each attendee was asked to bring a funny story about me or how they knew me. They were also asked to include a poem, song, prayer, or card that they would personally write for me as encouragement before surgery. As each friend received the invitation, they commented that it sparked energy and creativeness in them. It also sparked a common ground for each of us, because we all knew and loved someone with breast cancer. It sparked a sense of claiming our womanhood with each other.

The party was at my neighbor's home, the Johnson's. Jane had decorated her living and dining room with pink balloons, lovely pink flowers that filled the air with fragrance, and she had a large pink candle on the center of the coffee table that added ambiance to the room.

My daughter, Kimberly, opened the party with a welcome and the reason for our gathering, along with a few more specifics on my bi-lateral mastectomy, reconstruction, and following chemotherapy treatments. Kimberly, is the faithful daughter who had gone to all my doctor appointments with me and my husband Dick. She graciously offered to talk about the surgeries and other procedures I would have. Looking back, I cannot imagine how difficult this must have been for her. She informed the ladies that my surgery would include excising both breasts down to the chest wall and removing the latissimus dorsi muscles from the back to make new breast mounds. Six months of chemo would follow the surgery along with minor procedures they would be doing later.

Kimberly also shared research and history she had done on women and their breasts. My daughter is somewhat of an actor at parties, therefore some of what she shared brought tears to our eyes and some of her findings sent us into belly laughing, as we were all women who could identify with our breasts!

Then began our circle of breast sharing. One woman made signs of positive affirmations that were put up around the house. My dear friend Jean, whose creativity is endless, wrote an Ode to Joyce's Boobs with her husband, Lee, which she read at the party. Jean is an amazing friend and a music teacher at a local Christian school. While Jean is an extrovert, this poem took me by surprise, as I am sure they have never written anything like this before. We laughed and laughed as she read the poem!

The poem reads: To our friend Joyce by Lee and Jean DeVries

ODE TO HER BOOBS

I'll write a lovely ode
To the unusual load
That has for many years abode
On our dear Joyce for all to behold.
We speak of her voluptuous boobs
That looks nothing like a cube
Not even resembles a tube
For years they've bounced in JUBE-lation
They've given much pleasure to Dick, she's his wife
But now these boobs must meet the knife
She's had them for her entire life
So, let's hear a drum roll
And let's play the fife!
She's exchanging these boobs
For two perky hooters,
We're sure these two hooters
Will really suit her!
So, rally around Joyce,
You flutter and tooters
FOR WE ARE HER FRIENDS
AND GREATEST ROOTERS!"

My friend Mary sang a song from a tune from her heritage, "Swing Low Sweet Chariot" — the words went something like this:

"Swing Low, sweet breasts coming to carry Joyce to surgery!

Those sweet breasts will be no more but to new ones, we will soon attest!

Swing Low, no more, new perky ones she'll soon adorn!

At age 80 she'll still look good and the rest of us will probably hang low!"

After those two women's contributions, we all were belly-laughing until tears were rolling from our eyes and down our cheeks. One woman read a story about historically strong women who had faced a female crisis. Another woman shared stories about nurturing women and breast feeding as well as stories of women who had gone through breast cancer.

A friend read from the Song of Solomon and the beauty of fondling breasts and concluded with her thoughts that true beauty lies beneath the breasts. It is the woman you are on the inside that counts.

My dear daughter, Kimberly, then gave each woman a candle and asked them to light it on Monday morning while I was in surgery and to say a prayer for me at that time. (Little did they know that the candle would burn for about 11 hours of surgery time!) Kimberly then lit a unity candle as we took a moment of silence to remember all women who have had to face breast cancer and then read a prayer written by my dear friend Rev. Marchiene Rienstra.

Yes, in every season there is a time for laughing, a time for crying, a time for healing. This party night was a time to experience all of those emotions in a healthy, healing, joyful, compassionate way that would prepare me for surgery and beyond.

Of course, a party is never a party without dessert and favors! My friend, Jean, made two cakes shaped like breasts. One cake was chocolate and dense, into which we cut out a part of the cake representing the cancerous tumor and discarded that piece. She also had another booby cake that was fluffy and light representing my new model of breasts that were yet to be made.

We then sat around drinking tea, eating delicious cakes, and together made plaster molds of decorated boobies that I could display in the hospital room! For that, we blew up two pink balloons and spread plaster over them. We decorated the newly created plastered balloon boobies with sparkling jewels, good wishes, and pink feathers. We secured large brown buttons for the aurora and a pink jewel for the nipples! What a beautiful conversation piece this was hanging in my hospital room!

Yes, my breast had cancer, but my heart was full. That night I was laughed up, prayed up, and loved up enough to last anyone through surgeries, chemo, and the cancer journey. I had found one of the keys to healing through the laughter, love, and friendships of this party! I had said my goodbyes to my breasts. I had thanked God for the ways in which they had served me and now I was prepared for the new ones!

Now, I thought the rest would be a piece of cake! Ha-ha!

At the heart of this journey, I began to see the importance of using ritual in my healing process. From the beginning of time, we know that people throughout the world have used rituals for various occasions and rites of passage in order to add significance to their lives. A Bye, Bye Boobie Party is a means whereby ritual can help facilitate the richness and heritage we share as women whose breasts have held an important role in nurturing, lovemaking, and our womanhood.

As a woman who has had to say goodbye to her breasts, I began to realize the significance rituals play in this journey of loss. You see, it does not matter who we are on this journey of loss. It does not matter what body part we must lose to surgery. My journey became a lesson on learning to be grateful and thankful for the ways my breasts or body parts served me. Reciting a prayer or litany of gratitude became a ritual and a way for me to say goodbye to my breasts, in order to journey on.

Learning ways to say our goodbyes seems to make grief easier. This holds true for any difficult situation where one finds oneself. I also found how important it is to acknowledge what you are about to lose, journal about it, and then be thankful for the ways it served you. This was vital in my healing. Thankfulness in our loss helps us move on to surrender our bodies with humble gratefulness.

If you have been diagnosed with breast cancer and are facing a mastectomy, just imagine yourself at your own party, having to reflect on what your body has meant to you. Imagine being thankful for what it's given you, the joys of womanhood, and being a lover to someone special, the joys of nurturing and nursing a newborn. Those are joys that many women share. As you share the joys, within your special group of women you also share the sorrows, the grief, and the challenge as you maneuver through breast cancer, knowing you are supported and loved.

Imagine yourself at your own Bye, Bye Boobie party, being embraced by women, who love you. Imagine a time set aside specifically for your friends to celebrate and mourn with you. In fact, you will find that those close people you invited to share in your party will surround you with unfailing love. An evening like this will make your guests feel honored, to have been the ones chosen to share in this season of your life. Imagine yourself being lifted up by this energy of love, imagine yourself celebrating stories of your life that are healing, comforting, and bring laughter and cheer. Imagine yourself with your cheerleaders in life alongside you with prayers, songs, stories, words of wisdom, and rituals to share in your healing process. You see, our lives are meant to be shared, both our joys and our struggles.

Through the many hours spent visiting the sick in hospitals, as a chaplain and pastor, I observed that those who had a significant support system recovered much more readily than those with little or no support. Research also documents this.

That is why I immediately began enlisting my supporters to help ride this journey with me. It was out of this quest, that my Bye, Bye, Bobbie party was born. I have always been a person who loved engaging with people and enjoyed spontaneous fun. I knew that cancer was not something I enlisted for, but I was willing to learn from it and in turn help others to learn and heal as well.

Cancer became my teacher, as I prepared for this party. I would ask myself what I needed from this night in order to prepare for very major surgery and also to aid in my recovery process. I would find myself also wondering what other women might need, who found themselves facing not only breast cancer, but also mastectomies and reconstruction or loss of a body part. I found myself spending much time in prayer and meditation during this time, which I found essential to my well-being.

Suggestions for your own party:

BYE, BYE, BOOBIE PARTY CHECKLIST:
√ A party home
√ A host
√ Joyous, compassionate women
√ Bye, Bye, Boobie Invitations asking women to bring a poem, a song, a story, a prayer, and to share how they know the breast cancer patient.
√ Pink Balloons
√ Pink flowers
√ Affirmation cards, placed around the room
√ Glue
√ Plaster for the balloon decorating along with jewels, feathers
√ 2 Buttons and 2 pink jewels for nipples
√ Breast cakes
√ Tea or coffee, or wine

A side note: I know I have been gifted with great friends, many of whom are in ministry and medicine, but I want you to know that you too have friends who love you and want to participate in your healing.

If you are an invitee to a party, please don't be shy about sharing your prayers or words of encouragement. It will mean so much to the honored guest and all who attend. Remember, God, honors all prayers that come from the heart no matter who you are or what your age, so be brave enough to put your thoughts on paper.

To the honored guest, be vulnerable enough to receive these gifts with grace from your guests. You will be blessed and so will they!

SPECIAL SECTION:

QUESTIONS TO ASK YOUR HEALTH PROVIDER ABOUT SURGERY

Spectrum Health (now Corewell Health) gives their cancer patients a list of questions to ask about any cancer disease and treatment. As an active member of your health care team, you have the right to ask questions about your cancer and treatments. Spectrum Health's book gives a list of questions to ask your physicians and suggests you take notes.

SURGERY

- What kind of surgery can I consider?
- Which operation do you recommend for me?
- Will I need further treatment such as radiation or chemotherapy?
- Is it likely that I will need additional surgeries?
- How will I feel after surgery?
- Where will the scars be and what will they look like?
- Will I have to do special exercises before or after surgery?
- When can I get back to normal activities?

CHAPTER EIGHT

Surgery and its Aftermath

Even youths grow tired and weary,
and young men stumble and fall;
but those who hope in the Lord
will renew their strength.
They will soar on wings like eagles;
they will run and not grow weary,
they will walk and not faint.

— Isaiah 40:29-31

BESIDES THE PARTY, I HAD SEVERAL CONCERNS BEFORE I WENT UNDER the knife, to prepare to become comfortable in my literally-new skin.

About a week before surgery, life became busy with pre-admission testing, blood work, EKG, and chest X-Rays etc. My days and hours prior to surgery were spent in meditation, seeking God, and giving myself time to grieve and mourn my soon-to-be loss. It was a time of contemplation, a time for long walks, and coffee with special friends. It was a wonderful time to spend with my husband, holding hands and just being. Time spent in silence became golden.

Monday morning, my surgery day, found me in good spirits, rested, and ready to get the job done. During pre-surgery loved ones gathered by my bed: my dear and faithful husband Dick, my precious children, Kimberly, Jeffrey, and Joshua. Many of my dear pastoral friends, Pastors Lew, Eric, and Jan, Sister Sue, and colleagues joined us for prayer and support, as well as Dr. John and Rev. Marty Rienstra.

We all gathered hands around the bed and offered up prayers for surgery and wisdom for the doctors and those who would be part of the healing process. We prayed for every cell of my body to cooperate and to be revitalized by the healing energy of God.

I went into surgery knowing that with each breath I would take, divine energy would permeate every cell of my body and I would be free from fear and would begin the healing process on the wings of prayer! As we held hands and prayed, I felt a warm sensation of hope pulsating through my veins, as I was lifted up like the wings of eagles knowing that one day I would soar again! I felt eternally grateful for those who gathered with me that morning. It was a transformative moment, a gift of gratitude and grace. I was then off to la-la land!

The surgery lasted eleven hours and after I woke up, I realized immediately another test of perseverance was beginning as I was bandaged around my breasts and my back and there was absolutely no place to move without pain.

My surgeon Dr. D. and plastic surgeon Dr. H. had teamed up to not only do the bilateral mastectomy but also to begin the reconstruction process. Upon waking from the long procedure, I was overwhelmed by how battered and painful I felt across my entire body. I felt as if I had been in a war.

I did not realize how many muscle groups were involved within the chest, arm and back muscles. I did not realize how sore I would be from the latissimus dorsi muscles in my back being removed to reconstruct new breasts. I did not anticipate the pain of nerves being severed along with the surgery from the mastectomy. I was exhausted and groggy from the pain meds that made me sleepy.

I had asked my husband to limit my visitors to himself, our children, and Pastor Lew or Pastor Eric until I felt a bit stronger. From my role as a chaplain, I learned that post-surgery patients should not have too many visitors right away.

The next day, I was more alert and found a bit of improvement as I had been given doses of pain meds. The nurses educated me on my drain tubes. The drain tubes are inserted at the mastectomy site, armpits, and back where they removed the latissimus dorsi muscles. During surgery they insert drain tubes to allow excess blood and fluids that build up after surgery to drain. My husband and I were taught how to empty and clean them. The drain tubes felt very uncomfortable and annoying and my surgery area looked like it had been through a bloody war.

Waking up from surgery was not only extremely painful, but as I looked at myself, I wondered if any semblance of normal or beauty would ever occur. What once were breasts, were surgically excised or removed down to the chest wall and new breast mounds were created from the back latissimus dorci muscles. I felt ugly and gross.

Each time dressings were changed it was not only painful but just downright ugly. But aren't all wounds ugly, until they have time to heal, I would ask myself. My plastic surgeon said he was an artist in this form of reconstruction, but this art form looked so distorted to me and a wave of depression began to loom over me.

Then a voice within reminded me that any plastic surgeon can re-construct, but a good reconstructive surgeon is also a co-creator in restoring beauty. As a co-creator, they would do the surgery, but I was also a co-creator with them and God, as it was my job to remain positive about the reconstruction.

"After all, Joyce," the voice within reminded me, "If beauty doesn't radiate from within, no amount of reconstruction can ever recreate it. Seek the Divine in you, be a co-creator with the Divine and your inner beauty will determine your destiny. Fill your heart with gratitude that you were fortunate enough to have such good surgeons by your side."

Wow! Each time I needed an attitude adjustment, I began to thank God that all things are beautiful in their time. When I felt down, I kept reminding myself that I am a co-creator in this process, and I would begin to read positive affirmations I had put up around the house. I put on music that lifted my spirit. I would pray. I would read an inspiring story. I would watch a funny movie; I would call a special friend for encouragement. I did as much as I could to lift my spirits so that my divine inner spirit could radiate. Then, I knew I would begin to see the hand of the artist's work as I went through the long healing process. Yes, there is light at the end of the tunnel and beauty in the artist's hands.

When looking for an excellent plastic surgeon it is always important to look for a surgeon who is a co-creator in restoring beauty. Seek out their credentials, their distinguished awards, and recommendations from other people and ask to see pictures of their work. Do not be shy or intimidated by this; remember it's your body they will be working on.

Also remember that if beauty doesn't radiate from within, no amount of reconstruction can ever recreate beauty! So do your job by keeping positive and let the plastic surgeon do his or her job in reconstruction. They will be informative as to how you are looking and healing from surgery. They will be encouragers as they help their patients see beyond surgery to a new beginning and a positive self-image.

CHAPTER NINE

Treatment Strategies

But he said to me, "My grace is sufficient for you, for my power is made perfect in weakness." Therefore, I will boast all the more gladly of my weakness, so that Christ's power may rest on me.

— 2 Corinthians 12:9

DR. C. WAS MY ONCOLOGIST AND GUIDED ME THROUGH CHEMOTHERAPY. He is a kind gentleman and would spend quality time educating his patients and encouraging them on their journey. Chemotherapy is brutal, there is no other word than brutal. You and your doctor will discuss what treatments are necessary to ensure the cancer is gone from your body. Chemotherapy, radiation, or both. I had chemotherapy after the surgery with my first breast cancer and radiation after the surgery with my second breast cancer.

CHEMOTHERAPY

Chemotherapy is systemic and travels to every cell in your whole body, administering a variety of potent chemicals given through an IV, a port, or orally to destroy any cancer cells that might remain following surgery.

I had a port inserted under my skin on the upper chest to deliver my chemo drugs. This was much easier for me because of the many sessions of chemo I was to receive and because my veins are hard to access, and the drugs are hard on your veins. A cocktail of chemo drugs traveled through my bloodstream like a Pacman game gobbling up any bad cells in their way, before the cells had a chance to divide and multiply.

I had six months of treatments, which wiped me out. Occasionally my blood cells became immunosuppressed and immunocompromised and I was treated for anemia and bleeding tendencies. Chemo made me tired and I often felt like I had no energy. Chemo also brought on some depression, which I had to fight. I experienced some nausea which was helped by anti-nausea medication. I developed painful mouth sores as a result of the chemo. Just before each new chemo treatment I felt more energy and then another treatment would zap me.

Your blood cells need to regenerate each treatment cycle, or you won't be given the next treatment until your blood counts are back to normal. Before each treatment I sat among other patients waiting for my name to be called to draw blood. If my count was ok, then I could proceed with chemo, if not I would be given medication to bring my blood counts back to normal before chemo could be resumed. I often think the chemo was harder on me than all the surgery. With chemo there are many different drugs and often a cocktail of drugs that can have a variety of side effects on a person's body. It is important to become knowledgeable about the drugs you are given.

A difficult issue for me to deal with was hair loss. After my second chemo treatment all of my hair began to fall out. Hair loss due to chemotherapy affects all body hair, not only on my head but all over my body including my eyebrows and eyelashes, and you feel naked with hair loss.

I had always had blonde hair that was easy to manage. As a kid I was called Goldilocks by neighbors and enjoyed the nice comments on my long blonde curls. As an adult I wore my hair shorter and nicely styled. Losing my hair was a traumatic and dramatic change. Being bald makes you look different than you did before. You start looking like a cancer patient. I had always thought my head was rounder until the hair fell out and I discovered my head was oval.

I had to give myself several days to acquaint myself with my new look, but after a week or two I became somewhat accustomed to seeing myself bald. It was strange and funny to look in the mirror and wonder who that person was. When my hair first fell out, I was in the shower and as I washed my hair, it felt like ants crawling all over my head as the shower filled with hair. I often wore hats, because it was winter and covering up my head was helpful in removing the stigma that accompanies cancer. As spring and summer rolled on, I thought I would try a wig. If you are looking for a wig, the American Cancer Society and Gilda's club have good suggestions on where to purchase a wig.

I often wore my wig when I had to go to places and always wore it to church. One Sunday, someone accidentally brushed by me, and my wig shifted so much that I had to rearrange it. I smiled and laughed a bit and said, "Oh, the hazards of going bald!" The laughter took the tension off the person that had caused the incident and it made it easier to deal with. As hot summer days approached, sometimes wearing a wig was too hot, so I mostly wore a lightweight baseball hat which I felt good in.

I never knew I was so attached to my eyebrows and lashes until I had none. I felt so sparse, so plain. I did use an eyebrow pencil to make myself look better. I never did get the hang of fake eyelashes, so I wore sunglasses a lot, which helped. But I did not lose my happy smile and decided to replace my hair loss with smiles for people to look at and that made me feel better.

I found my skin to be drier during treatments so I would also moisturize my skin regularly. The last things to become weak or fall out were my fingernails and toenails. So, there you have it, no hair, no brows or lashes, no nails, but I had my smile and no one or anything could take that away! When my hair did come in after chemo, it came in wavy and platinum blonde. It is really quite lovely and a real treat to have back. Thank you, God!

Be assured by your hair loss that the chemotherapy is affecting dividing cells, including your cancer cells, and all is working to eliminate the cancer.

RADIATION

Radiation is localized to destroy cancer within the body with carefully aimed beams of radiation. Radiation is intended to eliminate any stray cells left behind from surgery because even if your margins are clear, there could be some stray cells that need to be zapped. Radiation is a high-intensity x-ray that kills rapidly dividing cells while allowing regular cells to do their own job and not destroy the good cells.

Your radiation oncologist determines the number of treatments and the area to be treated. Radiation was much easier on my body than chemo. I had 40 rounds of radiation.

SPECIAL SECTION:

QUESTIONS TO ASK YOUR HEALTH PROVIDER ABOUT TREATMENTS

Spectrum Health (now Corewell Health) gives their cancer patients a list of questions to ask about any cancer disease and treatment. As an active member of your health care team, you have the right to ask questions about your cancer and treatments. Spectrum Health's book gives a list of questions to ask your physicians and suggests you take notes.

CHEMOTHERAPY

- What medicines will I be taking? How often? How long? What do they do?
- Will I lose my hair?
- How will I feel during chemotherapy?
- Can I continue to work?
- What happens if I miss a dose?
- Can I take other medications during treatment? Can I continue herbal supplements?
- Can I drink alcoholic beverages during treatment?
- What are the restrictions to my normal daily activities?

RADIATION

- How will the radiation be given?
- How many treatments will I get? Over what period of time?
- When will the treatment begin?
- When will it end?
- Will I need hormonal treatment? How long will each treatment take to receive?
- Can I schedule treatments at certain times of the day?
- How will I know if the radiation is working?
- What side effects should I expect?

- Will I lose my hair?
- Will I need to take any special precautions?
- Will I need a special diet?
- Can I continue to take herbal supplements?
- What happens if I miss a treatment?
- What are the restrictions to my normal daily activities?

HORMONE THERAPY

- Why do I need this treatment?
- What medicines will I be taking? How often? How long? What will they do?
- Which would be better for me, medicine or an operation?
- How long will I be on this treatment?

(My sincere thanks to Spectrum Health, now Corewell Health for these helpful checklists and information.)

CHAPTER TEN

Dealing with Setbacks

Praise the Lord, my soul;
all my inmost being, praise his holy name.
Praise the Lord, my soul,
and forget not all his benefits—
who forgives all your sins
and heals all your diseases,
who redeems your life from the pit
and crowns you with love and compassion,
who satisfies your desires with good things
so that your youth is renewed like the eagle's.

— Psalm 103:1-5

DURING MY MASTECTOMY SURGERY, 28 LYMPH NODES WERE REMOVED. This process is known as an "axillary node dissection" or "sentinel node dissection." The lymph nodes are part of the lymphatic system which is responsible for removing toxins and cleansing the body.

Removal of lymph nodes provides information to your oncologist as to what type of treatment will be required beyond surgery. If breast cancer has spread to other parts of the body, it will do so by traveling through the bloodstream or lymph nodes. With breast cancer, the lymph nodes from the chest, if found positive, allow the cancer to travel through the armpit before traveling to other areas of the body. If no positive cancer cells are found in the lymph nodes the cancer is contained and has not traveled to other areas of the body. So, you can understand why the axillary node dissection is so important.

To my delight, my nodes were not positive, meaning the cancer had not spread to other areas of the body.

However, there were long term implications of lymphedema. After surgery and for many years later I lost feeling in my upper arm and armpit because the sensory nerves were severed during surgery in order to get the lymph node samples. Along with that I had no feeling in my back where the nerves were severed from where the latissimus dorsi muscles were removed to be used to build new breast mounds. I pretty much felt numb in the front and back, for years, a very weird feeling.

Lymphedema swelling has been a constant and scary result of lymph node dissection for me, causing near death experiences when cellulitis would develop leading to sepsis. Lymphedema swelling is due to blockage of the lymphatic vessels, most often due to surgery or radiation therapy that damages these vessels and leads to poor drainage in the absence of lymph nodes.

There was a time when my husband and I took a helicopter ride in Sedona, Arizona. Because of the elevation, my arm turned bright red and swelled like an elephant leg! I developed cellulitis which quickly turned to sepsis and was hospitalized for five days on IV antibiotics.

After that episode, I was fitted for a lymphedema compression sleeve which I always wear when flying. I wear a compression sleeve to prevent bug bites or pricks from rose bushes while gardening. Any bug bite, puncture, or too much sun makes one a candidate for lymphedema to quickly turn to cellulitis.

Another time, my husband and I were hiking the national parks in Utah. I had worn my sleeve hiking, but a bug bit my arm sometime when I was sleeping in a hotel at Bryce Canyon National Park. The next day, as happened before, my arm was pink and somewhat swollen. We were driving to our son's house in Los Angeles, California that day. By the time we got there my hand, arm and shoulder were bright red, and swollen like an elephant leg. I developed a high fever and chills and was really quite sick. We probably should have stopped at a hospital on the way to his house, but I was intent on getting there. My son called his friend, Dr. Prudence Hall and she said to go straight to Cedar Sinai Hospital. I was immediately admitted as I developed sepsis again and was hospitalized for a week. Unfortunately, this happens so quickly that it becomes life-threatening. Lymphedema must be taken seriously.

If lymphedema is an issue for you, be sure to ask your doctor for a prescription for a compression sleeve. Physical therapy is also very helpful in reducing swelling. To help prevent lymphedema, keep your skin well moisturized, and avoid getting cuts, bites, sunburns, shots and blood pressure readings in the affected arm.

If you are to have lymph nodes removed, be diligent in doing your research on lymphedema as a preventive measure. With all the information that is given to a cancer patient, I do not remember being told much about the long-term implications of lymphedema until it affected me. If you develop a red heat and swelling in your arm, pain, fever, or chills it would be wise to call your doctor immediately.

About six weeks later as mentioned before, the lymphedema occurred again in Grand Rapids. This time at Spectrum Hospital they did a PET scan and found that my cancer had returned and was under the chest wall where they had removed the breasts.

For more information you can visit www.lymphnet.org or call 800.541.3259. If you live near Grand Rapids, Mi Spectrum Health, (Corewell Health) Lemmen Holden Cancer Center has an excellent Physical Therapy program that deals with lymphedema.

Post-chemo, I was placed on oral anti-cancer fighting drugs. These drugs ate away at my bones, making them brittle and my joints were inflamed with much pain. I had difficulty healing from a fall. I have considerable pain in my joints which I believe may be due to these drugs.

I took myself off the drugs in order to have a better quality of life. I found there are times when quality of life is more important than quantity. I only mention this because after going through chemotherapy, I was put on oral drugs as a preventative measure of cancer recurrence and experienced bad side effects. Please be aware of any side effects from medications, do your research, and talk over any difficulties with your doctor before you have complications!

PART TWO

HELP FOR MY FELLOW TRAVELERS

CHAPTER ELEVEN

Fears and Anxiety

> In their book *Living With Loss,* Dr. Ronald Ramsey and Rene Noorbergen suggest that the moment a woman finds she has breast cancer, she is often reeling from some degree of fear, paralysis, stress and anxiety. The sense of shock persists in the woman until after surgery, when she realizes it was indeed cancer and that one or both of her breasts had been removed. It takes several days for the shock to pass and the patient can endure many conflicting and confusing emotions until it is overcome. Fear is a component that accompanies breast cancer and even the possibility of dying of cancer is real. Fear that her husband no longer desires her sexually, fear that he looks at another woman and feels cheated or is looking for another partner.
>
> Dr. Ronald Ramsay and Rene Noorbergen,
> *Living with Loss, pg 198*

ONE OF MY GREATEST FEARS FROM MY MASTECTOMY AND reconstruction was that my body would look disfigured or lopsided. Around and around my mind would spin, dwelling on how I would look or feel or if people would look at me and see me as incomplete.

Ramsay and Noorbergen suggest that a woman may often feel incomplete following a mastectomy and that these strong feelings often bring about fear and can almost paralyze a woman if she dwells on her fears. If she does not come to grips with her self-worth, fear will continue to paralyze her." She must see herself as worthy, a woman with potential, a gem, a pearl of great price who still has much value and love to give to those she loves and a world that still needs her.

I was blessed because my family always would remind me how important I was to them. It seemed their love for me grew even stronger since cancer and I know my love for them surely did! My love for God also grew so much stronger than before cancer, as I learned to lean on God daily.

Ramsey and Noorbergen also suggest in their book *Living with Loss*:

Most people shy away from discussing cancer, particularly when someone has undergone major surgery. Additionally, the matter will remain buried if the post-mastectomy patient avoids interaction with others in her immediate vicinity (family, friends, co-workers) because she feels humiliated or embarrassed by her loss. Her repressed feelings won't be able to express themselves or have a chance to die down. As a type of denial, withholding the excruciating pain, sadness, fear, and worries is something she struggles with throughout the bereavement process. The patient must open up and share with others around her. Only by discussing and weighing the advantages and disadvantages of the new life will the patient find lasting happiness.

My suggestion is to find others with a common lot to share your concerns. Throughout my cancer journey, I spent many days visiting Gilda's Club. Gilda's Club offers many activities and classes and they are a blessing and helpful in dealing with cancer issues that come up during a time such as this. They offer classes on various types of cancers bringing in doctors that speak on various topics in their areas of specialties. They have grief and bereavement support groups, a wonderful and informative library, a kids club, meals that are served on various days, dietitians, and various classes such as art, computer, and knitting taught by volunteers.

Often, I would take comedy videos to watch at Gilda's club with my cancer sisters. I realized one of the key ingredients missing in dealing with cancer was the ability to laugh and release some of those endorphins.

You may ask, what do you mean by laughing when dealing with a serious issue? Genuine laughter provides physical and psychological benefits, releases tension, and lightens oppressive situations. Laughter seemed to be one of the key ingredients I needed to keep going, moving ahead and healing. I would fill many evenings watching comedy movies, reading a good book or funny story, and journaling. I knew the old adage that laughter is the best medicine would be key in my healing process.

As I visited Gilda's Club, I began to realize how serious so many of the cancer patients' diagnoses were. I experienced the vital need for such a safe place for cancer patients to gather and open up with sisters who have been where you are. Gilda's support groups help patients to find ways to cope with their illness, to meet with others who are dealing with cancer and to talk about your fears and problems as well as finding advice and counsel. It is a place where you can share your feelings confidentially, as well as a place of encouragement and a place to share your victories.

Cancer patients often ask the question, "Why me? This just can't be! How could God let this happen?" It is then the journey of coming to terms with your loss and grief becomes reality as we face the truth of what has happened to our body. This may be a good time to get involved in a support group or and find a professional counselor who will listen to your story and help you to process what has happened.

You will also find your oncology nurse navigator to be helpful and resourceful. Sometimes just being able to put one foot in front of the other is your most difficult task, so it is important to have that other person in your life to help you navigate so you do not feel alone.

There are no shortcuts to grief or your loss, so here are some important steps to consider.

- Own your own experience, it is unique to you.
- Take the steps towards healing even when it is very painful
- Confide in someone, join a support group
- Exercise
- Release your anger
- Avoid chemical dependency
- Meditate
- Find rituals that may help
- Listen to soothing music

- Try doing some artwork that represents where you are and where you want to be.
- And last but not least, exercise your faith through prayer, scripture, meditation and being honest with God.

Being honest with God pays big dividends. God already knows our situation and how we are feeling, so put your feelings into words and ask for help. God is eager to help and enter our pain and bring us on the road to wellness. God is only a blink away, just ask.

The Reach to Recovery program is another organization to consider. I stayed with Gilda's Club because it was close to home and I loved the setting and the safe welcoming environment!

Spectrum Health Lemmen Holton Cancer Center, in Grand Rapids, is also an interesting avenue. I joined their music and art therapy classes and found it to be a helpful way to reduce stress, to be creative and to take my mind off myself. Many hospitals offer programs such as these, so be sure to ask your oncology nurse navigator if your hospital offers such programs. I felt blessed to have such a fine oncology center as the Lemmen Holton Cancer Center close to home. As I think of the many programs that are offered to cancer patients, I want to acknowledge and give thanks to the many philanthropy donors who make programs such as these possible!

When dealing with cancer there are women who do not identify or can't open up about their cancer often because of shame — shame that they are not a complete woman, shame that they perhaps contributed to this disease through their lifestyle. Whatever the issues are that are producing elements of shame, I say loudly, stop it! There is no shame in cancer!

Please, if you are feeling shame, see a counselor that specializes in shame. Read the works of Brené Brown on shame. Work on your issues so that you can proceed on your cancer journey to wellness.

CHAPTER TWELVE

Surrendering Fear

Lord my God, I called you for help and you healed me.

— Psalm 30:2

I HAD AN INSPIRING EXPERIENCE DURING MY WESTERN THEOLOGICAL Seminary days while on a trip to El Salvador and Nicaragua during the ten-year war. The people in those poor countries lived under horrible oppression of the government then in power. There was much loss of land and the torture of so many loved ones during the war. Yet, these people learned to live with gratitude for even the smallest things. They knew the power of living in community with love for one another and sharing the little of what they had with each other.

Their actions of giving up their lives for others spoke volumes about love in the midst of oppression. They learned to be brave people and to fight against oppression. Their fears were replaced with a cause for freedom and love. The words of Scripture became flesh and dwelt among them, as they heard the words "Do not be afraid, for I am with you, I will fight your battles with you. Do not fear, for I am with you, do not be dismayed, for I am your God. I will strengthen you and help you; I will uphold you with my right hand." Isaiah 41:10-13

Pray, as you read these words, that you too, will surrender your fears to the one who says "Do not be afraid." Fear can immobilize us and cast us into doubt and depression. Doubt has the power to mislead us and zap the joy from us. Fear and doubt are very powerful and make us question everything and destroy our self-confidence. Fear is a paralysis that keeps us from moving forward and fear keeps us from experiencing peace. When we deal with our fears, they cease to control us, and we become free to deal with what lies ahead of us.

Time after time, the word of the Lord came to people who were afraid: reassuring them to not be afraid, that He is with us, He is our strength, our help, our shield, He is the one who can see us through anything and can give us comfort and peace.

Even if you are not healed from your cancer or another disease, know that God's loving presence is there and He promises to hold onto us and give us strength.

As we release the fears of our illness to the God of compassion, you will then be able to fight your battle knowing that the God who goes before you, will also be in the battle with you. As Christ goes before you notice how fear begins to dissipate. As fear loses its hold and you are lifted by Spirit's love you will be able to fight cancer with courage.

It is the peace of Christ's presence in the midst of fear and suffering that develops faith. It is faith that gives us the courage to fight our battles. Faith is a decision to act according to the promises of God who loves us and walks with us encouraging us in our struggles. This faith sometimes is a minute-by-minute, hour-by-hour, day-by-day decisions to trust God. Remember, He hears our every prayer, shares in our tears, and wraps us in His loving arms and whispers life-giving words of love, encouragement, and resurrection power. The God of the Hebrew Scriptures says, "I set before you life and death, blessing and curse, therefore choose life. that both you and your seed will live." Deuteronomy 30:19

I would encourage you to keep a journal and list your fears. Ask yourself how your fears paralyze you. Talk to God about your fears and ask Him to enfold you in His love until all of your fears melt like butter. Take time to meditate and be still before the Divine and ask what you need to change in order to bring your life into alignment with the perfect will of God, in order to prosper and be in good health and to be a person of love and compassion.

As you fight your own battle with cancer, often compassion becomes your companion on the journey. In fact, the word compassion literally means to weep with. The Bible talks about Jesus weeping. Jesus was called by Mary and Martha to the tomb of their brother Lazarus, where a crowd stood weeping. Seeing them weep, Jesus was moved with compassion and shared in their tears and wept with them, even though He knew He could restore Lazarus.

The God who chooses to live and die with us, the God who shares in our common lot, the God who weeps over our sufferings, is the same God who knows when we face the difficult words: You have cancer. He weeps with us and walks with us.

The God who weeps over injustice, poverty, oppression, sickness, and infirmities is the one who says, "I will never leave you or forsake you." Deuteronomy 31:8

The God who says, "Come unto me, all who are weary and burdened and I will give you rest." Matthew 11:28

The God who takes the yoke of our burdens is the Jesus who suffered and died a horrendous death for us. Because he suffered such pain, he can enter our pain. You see, it is Jesus who suffers with us, it is Jesus, who shares in our sorrows and pain and weeps with us. He knows us in our loneliness as our heart breaks. He knows us. He has been there. He has suffered the horrendous pain of the cross. Therefore, He feels our pain and chooses to walk with us, to be our comforter, to be the Compassionate One on our journey. He is the one who can transform us, the one who can be our companion through whatever we suffer and can turn our mourning into joy.

This is also the God who calls on believers to be Jesus with skin on and to be the compassionate healers of all who suffer from illness, death and loss, infirmities, depression, oppression, injustice and bringing in the reign of God's love and peace to those who suffer.

As we walk in compassionate ways, we share in the oneness of God and bless the world. As we are transformed by this amazing love energy, we become strengthened, empowered, and free. Out of nothing, we become something, reborn in love, created in love, mended in love!

And these dry bones once again live!

CHAPTER THIRTEEN

Some Prayers to Help You

The LORD is my shepherd;
I shall not want.
He makes me lie down in green pastures;
He leads me beside quiet waters.
He restores my soul;
He guides me in the paths of righteousness
for the sake of His name.
Even though I walk through the valley of the shadow of death,
I will fear no evil,
for You are with me;
Your rod and Your staff, they comfort me.
You prepare a table before me
in the presence of my enemies.
You anoint my head with oil;
my cup overflows.
Surely goodness and mercy will follow me
all the days of my life,
and I will dwell in the house of the LORD
forever.

— Psalm 23

PRAYING SCRIPTURE BACK TO GOD IS A WONDERFUL WAY TO FOCUS ON his promises and provisions. You can pray verses out loud over your life, over your sickness, and your loved ones. I suggest starting with Psalm 23. or use a scripture that is meaningful to you. Pray your prayer in first person pronoun and personalize it. Write your prayer down for future use.

I have written some additional prayers for you. I have prayed these prayers during my illness and they have built my faith, strengthened my soul and I have found healing.

I hope these prayers will help and strengthen you.

PRAYERS FOR HEALING.

Gracious God, whose faithful love endures and whose mercies never cease. Great is your faithfulness in desiring to give us hope and a future free from disease and infirmities. Please help me to keep my focus on you when pain and hurt are overwhelming. Help me to be faithful and to see the good and blessings that are all around me and to be truly grateful. Please strengthen my mind, body, and spirit and heal me, I pray. I stand firm on your words of healing for me. In Mark 5:34 we are told the story of a woman who had been bleeding for twelve years. She believed if she would just touch the hem of your garment she would be healed. She touched your garment, Jesus, and was instantly healed. Your response to her was, daughter, your faith has made you well, go in peace and be healed of your diseases. God, please give me that healing faith today.

Creator God, I praise you that I am fearfully and wonderfully made. I believe that your life-giving power flows to every cell of my body revitalizing every part of me until it is in perfect alignment and will function, as you created it to be. Please, reveal and release any spirit of unforgiveness, bitterness, anger, trauma, resentments or the spirit of death that I have held in my heart. I renounce any unclean spirit and command it to leave my body in Jesus name. I break the power of any evil spirit or generational sins and curses that may have caused harm, confusion or illness in my body. I call forth the release of the Holy Spirit to heal and direct my life. Forgive me of my sins and bring to remembrance those I need to forgive so that we can all be whole and live happy lives.

I give my angels charge over me to keep me strong, renewed and protected as I seek the healing hand of the Great Physician to do His work in my life. I call forth a release of the Holy Spirit to be active in my life, filling my body with divine healing energy, penetrating into every cell and fiber of my being. I declare and visualize every abnormal cell being eaten up like pac-men until there is no fertile ground for the cancer to grow or metastasize. Lord, as I pray, I feel a great calming wave of your warm healing spirit running through my veins, revitalizing my energy, filling my body as you touch and make me whole. Thank you, thank you, for your healing energy that is infusing my body. Great is your love for me!

God, I am so grateful that you are with me on this cancer journey and I thank you for the good and blessings that will come out of this experience. May I use this journey to be a blessing to others, to be the wounded healer in another person's life. Giver of Life, today I choose to see myself the way you see me, whole and well as I bathe in your healing oil and pure waters, trusting in you for recovery, as you Great Physician, make all things new.

God, I have prayed for my own healing, now please strengthen and give endurance to all those who are undergoing surgeries, chemo, radiation treatments and experimental drugs so that they too, may experience the miracle of your healing love and hear the words, your cancer is in remission. All is well. Help us to be good stewards of our bodies and lifestyles, to strengthen them with nutrition, rest, mental, emotional and spiritual health. Give strength to all of our families and loved ones as they walk this journey with us. We are so very grateful for them. Thank you, God, for all the ways you have blessed me and have been with me on this journey. I walk by faith with a grateful heart believing all is well! To God be the glory!

In Jesus Name,
Amen

A PRAYER FOR PHYSICIANS, NURSES, MEDICAL STAFF, RESEARCHERS AND CAREGIVERS.

Holy Spirit, please reveal a cure for cancer, as there are so many who suffer from the enemy of this disease. I ask for a release of wisdom and knowledge for cancer researchers as they perform their cancer studies. Lord, there is so much divine health that you have placed in the garden of earth. Please reveal more holistic approaches to our researchers, so they develop more natural approaches to medicine.

I thank you for our physicians, oncologists, nurses and medical staff who labor so intensively to bring us health. Please bless them and grant to them healthy bodies, strength and wisdom, in all they do for their task is daunting.

I thank you too for all the philanthropic donors to cancer research, hospitals and patient care. Bless them for their generous hearts, because without their financial help cancer research would be limited.

Help us to be good stewards of our bodies and lifestyles, with proper nutrition, rest, mental and emotional alertness and spiritual health. Give strength and encouragement to families who are our caregivers please. Thank you to all who stand with cancer patients on their journey, pastors, chaplains, church members, neighbors and especially dear family and friends as they make our journey's lighter and bring hope to our paths. Bless and give strength to all who care for us, as we are so grateful for them.

Above all God, I am so grateful that you go before me on this cancer journey. God you are my rock, my sure foundation, the One I trust to see me through dark days into the light. You are the one who will use my trials and life lessons to bless others on their journey. Thank you that you never leave me alone and are always by my side dear Lord.

Giver of Life, I choose to see myself as you see me, whole and well as I step into your healing energy and bathe in your healing oil and pure waters, trusting you for recovery as you make all things new.

Thank you, God, for all the ways you have loved me on this journey. I walk by faith, believing, All Will Be Well! To God be the glory!

Amen.

MINUTE PRAYERS

Sometimes when we are dealing with cancer and the pain is great, we are exhausted. All we are able to do is to say a minute prayer. I have written these with hopes that they may be helpful to you.

1. Loving and gracious God, touch me now with your healing hands. I believe that your will is for me to be well in mind, body and spirit. Cover me under the wings of your protection and heal me I pray. Help me to visualize every abnormal cell dying at its root, until there are no abnormal cells left to enter my bloodstream or lymphatic system. Keep me strong so that your healing flows through me cleansing my body and making all things new. Amen.

2. Loving God, my heart is heavy and I so desperately need you. I need you to give me courage, when I am discouraged. Lord, give me courage to keep praying, even when I doubt your presence and wonder if you even hear my requests. I ask for healing for my body and to let me feel safe in your presence. Help me to believe that you are still good, even when my journey is rough. May I rest myself in your good hands, my healer and comforter. Amen.

3. Lord, I thank you that You are Jehovah Rapha, the God who heals. Right now, I am weak and tired and worn out from surgeries and treatments for cancer. I am lonely and somewhat fearful about the future. Lord, you have promised to never leave me alone, you have assured me that you are by my side, sharing in my tears and encouraging me. Today, may I feel your presence as you restore me through your healing touch. Amen.

4. Gracious God, I need you to be my rock as I navigate through the trials of cancer. I am so thankful that I do not have to face these trials alone, that you are with me, giving me courage. Thank you for my family, friends and church family who stand with me. Bless my physicians and me with wisdom and discernment regarding my health. I surrender my life and my concerns to you and believe you will supply all I need to heal and be whole. Amen.

5. God, I look into the mirror and see the way this ravaging disease has eaten away at my body. Sometimes, I barely recognize my reflection. I know this body is only temporary and for the days that remain for me, may I be a reflection of your love and grace. As I reach the end of this life on earth, fill me with peace and contentment that You are my hope and will one day call me to yourself. I long to be worshiping you in the perfect heavenly body that You have waiting for me. So, until I see you face to

face, I will bless you, Lord of light, the God of my salvation. Amen.

6. Lord, have mercy.

7. Prayer for Protection (Unity Prayer of Protection)

   Prayed over me by Marty Rienstra during my recent hospitalization for Spinal Surgery.
   The light of God,
   surrounds us,
   The love of God enfolds us;
   The power of God
   protects us;
   The presence of God
   watches over us;
   Wherever we are,
   God is! (And all is well!)

I also would like to include a section of the book *Swallows Nest* written by my dear friend, Rev. Marchiene Rienstra.

Psalm 102 This may be a prayer for a woman suffering from a serious disease.

El Shaddai, hear my cry, and let my prayer come home to Your heart. Do not hide Your face from me in my distress. Open Your ears to my call and answer me quickly. For my days dwindle like smoke, and my bones ache and burn. My heart withers within me like mown grass. I forget to eat my food. When I groan loudly, my flesh strains against my bones. I am like an owl in the wilderness, an owl which lives in the desert.

I keep my lonely watch like a solitary bird on a housetop. All day long this enemy of disease ravages my well-being. Food tastes like ashes, and I mingle my tears with my drink. Why has this happened? Are you angry with me? It seems you have abandoned me, have cruelly tossed me away. My days are like a fleeting shadow. I wither away like cut wild flowers.

But You, El Shaddai, live forever.
Every generation remembers You.
Will You arise and have mercy on me?
Has the time of your favor come?
You have broken my strength in midlife!
Your hand has shortened my days.
Oh God, do not take me away from this life so soon,
You whose years last through all generations.

You founded the earth in ages past.
The heavens are your handiwork.
Though they will perish, You will endure.
They will wear out like old clothes,
And you will change them like garments.
But your years have no end.

Nations of the earth, rulers of the earth,
Stand and revere God's name!
For she builds up her people in strength,
And appears among them in glory.
She listens to the pleas of the destitute.
She takes their petitions to heart.
From her holy outlook, she sees the whole earth,
And hears all those who groan in pain.
She sets free those who are doomed to die,
So that they may proclaim Her name,
So that they may sing Her praise when the people gather in worship.

Benediction:
May God bless and nourish us and all who are in need today
With her strength in our weakness,
With her compassion in our failure,
With her comfort in our distress.
Amen.
Marchiene Rienstra, Swallows Nest

CHAPTER FOURTEEN

When Grief is a Friend

I think grief exposes us to our weakness. I think the feeling of grief tells us the power of trauma over our history. I think it tells us how vulnerable we are. I think it tells us the bond that each of us have because we are human. Because we are humane, we suffer. Because we are human, we have tears to cry. Because we are human our hearts are broken. Because we are human, we understand that loss is a common language. Everyone mourns. We all have failures and broken dreams. We all have broken relationships. We all encounter health issues at some point in our lives and have bodies that don't function the way they used to. Although grief is personal, everybody grieves.

Paraphrased summary of a sermon by Rev.
Dr. Jacqui Lewis @middlechurch.com.

Our cancer journey will have elements of grief. It is a traumatic event. Be aware, each person's grief is unique to themselves and will vary in depth throughout the journey. It is important to realize how vital it is to have someone present to share and to validate your grief. I think it is important to be a good listener and to be present to the grieving, without trying to point out the silver lining of suffering. The gift of presence is one of the most precious gifts someone can receive when going through trials. So when possible, be the friend that gives the gift of presence to someone in need. The gift of presence involves putting your needs aside to just be present and listen to another's needs. Words are not nearly as important as a listening, compassionate ear.

I believe each person must learn to deal with their grief in their own way and their own time. Grief can include feelings of shock when one receives the news, "You have cancer," then numbness and disbelief may set in. Grief can send shockwaves through your body rattling the foundation of our lives if we do not let the anger find a way out. Grief can find its way to the interior of our body, creating a storm of anger in our spirit, nearly devouring us.

Eventually, the anger breaks away and we may feel a depth of sadness, a sadness that never seems to go away and keeps gnawing away at you. This sadness can reach way down inside your mind, body and spirit and you may feel as if you are drowning. Every time you try to take a breath, it seems to pull you under with the next wave. There may be tears that just don't want to stop and little unexpected things can turn the waterfalls on. You may feel as if you are in a fog unable to find your way out. This is a time when we must be careful and seek help as this sadness can lead to depression eating away at our flesh and bones. The sadness will remain until you find a way to calm the storm and begin the healing process. That is why seeking the help from a counselor or pastor is essential in discovering tools to help bring you out of your sadness or depression. This is a time when you can invite the comfort from the Holy Spirit to begin wrapping warm love around you and drying your tears.

As we surrender to our grief and pain, healing takes place and begins to mend our tired body. and wrapping a blanket of love around us ensuring that we are safe and validated. This is a time when our tears become the balm for our wounds and oil for our soul gently massaging and mending and nurturing us back to wholeness. Eventually, we can validate that the pain we experienced was real and not to be forgotten and we can move on with the grace of God beside us to direct and guide us. Grief no longer swallows us up and the tears begin to lessen. This is when we can begin to feel as if we can allow our scars to turn to stars, as we have learned what grief has taught us. This is a time when we can eventually let the soft and gentle rain cleanse us as we move beyond grief to once again experiencing the beauty of life.

Along with grief there is so much information for a cancer patient to take in. During this time a person may have an inability to concentrate or be forgetful. I suggest always taking notes when you go to an appointment, or better yet take another person along to take notes or record your appointment.

Dealing with grief and your emotions is another avenue where Gilda's Club can help you to vent and understand why you are feeling the way you do. Grief symptoms are part of our body's instinct for survival called fight or flight. Just because I deal with my grief one way, does not mean you need to do the same thing. Grief is not a rule book, just as each of us are unique people, so our grief is uniquely our own. While there are common things we share in grief, we should honor our own experience and not compare it to someone else.

Grief and the way we process it takes as long as it takes for each individual. Grief is not something we can hurry through. Give yourself time and be gentle and patient with yourself. Rest as much as you are able, as grief often seems to be endless, and the weight of grief crushing and exhausting. Remember each person deals with grief in their own way and their own time.

And while the weight of grief may seem crushing, with time and acceptance of what has happened to us, that grief can prepare us for something beautiful. You see, in our breaking, in our tears, we learn to surrender to the Divine and that gives us hope, which is a pathway to becoming whole. With hope even our deepest wounds have meaning. All the traumas, all the pain, all the betrayals, all the disappointments can become like fertile fields when hope is present. As we allow ourselves to become vulnerable and surrender to pain and grief it takes us to a place where wisdom and faith is grown. It takes us to a resting place in Christ where our hopes are renewed and we can believe in healing. This path isn't just preparing us to be healed, it is preparing us to be healers as well and once that truth fills us, hopelessness dissipates like a mist.

That is when we know we have been transformed. We will still miss our loved ones who have gone before us. We may still have questions of why a lingering illness invaded our lives, but as hope fills our hearts, we will find that we no longer grieve as we once did. Instead, we fill our lives with precious memories, hope and a sense of purpose as we become wounded healers for another person. When we become transformed in this way, we are now ready to wrap our arms around the next grieving soul, offer them grace, and find comfort in all the tenderness those moments will hold.

In my times of grief, I experienced anger and sadness. I found that as I surrendered my pain to God, I was able to experience God's grace and healing which carried me through my loss. Grief has its own timetable for each of us. Grief is a journey, a process, a passageway through our darkness into surrender, wrapped in the loving arms of God. Hope is the greatest gift God gives to survive our pain. I grieved with hope. I grieved with hope of a better tomorrow, a hope of a time when there will be no more illness or no separation from loved ones, a hope with a beautiful heavenly future that God in His grace has prepared for us.

Over the years, I have found that as I draw near to grief, so too do I move beyond grief. Suffering then becomes a friend, a friend connected to love and to our eternal hope. Grief becomes my teacher, my advisor, my counselor, my hope, my wisdom and eventually my joy. Grief becomes my partner as I become the wounded healer to others who are hurting.

Paraphrasing C.S. Lewis from his book A Grief Observed, Lewis suggests that grief and love are the costs associated with unconditional love and dedication we have for another person as humans. When we lose the person we love, it hurts us more deeply the more we love them. But if we were completely truthful, would we want it any other way?

Experiencing loss is a very painful process with many tears. It is my hope that any insights in this book may be helpful. It is my hope that you will find that special person to vent with, those special people to cry with. Sometimes crying is something you do with others, other times it is something you do by yourself. Sometimes crying comes in unexpected ways and waves, but cry and let it out. We all need to cry; it is a God-given therapy and as you shed your tears you will find some release.

To paraphrase a quote by Washington Irving he suggests that tears have a sacred quality, they don't signify powerlessness, but strength instead. They communicate more effectively than hundreds of words. They carry messages of utter sorrow, profound contrition and unfathomable love. Isn't that wonderful!

As a pastor I would sit by the bedside of someone suffering from an incurable illness or beside the family grieving the loss of a loved one, their tears would mingle together with mine and God's as we would pray together. I have found that sitting with people in their hours of need is a sacred place and a place where tears are honored.

I believe we must honor our tears and as we allow our tears to flow, remember God shares in our tears and understands our emotions, and is able to also dry our tears with a towel of compassion. Inviting God into our grief means we will never walk alone.

In our suffering, our illness, our grief, God is not a distant spectator, but is involved in our pain and disappointments and sorrows. God shares in our pain and our tears. When our hearts are broken, so God shares in our brokenness, drawing us close, embracing our woundedness and encouraging our oneness with him. Surrendering to this divine power in our illness makes a very real difference in how we deal with life, giving us eternal purpose and hope.

So, I bless you with peace as you process whatever news you receive from your oncologist or doctor. As you face your illness, I pray that you will have family and community that can stand alongside encouraging you. Today, I bless you with the gift of presence, the gift of courage and encouragement from someone who cares. May you experience the peace of Christ in all your ways on this journey.

Through the Storm

Throughout life's daily walk,
There are drops of rain, and sometimes torrential storms,
In life's ever flowing journey,
There are days of sunshine and also painful storms.

Sometimes the storms of life
Come to each one.
During that time of darkness,
We cannot see the sun.
Crying out to God for help,
He assures me He is near,
And helps to calm my deepest fears.

And while the strong winds blow,
And the tempest is near,
I walk through the storm with confident faith,
That a rainbow will appear,
And all will be well.

And so it is, when our faith is tried,
We are humbled,
We are tired.
We seek forgiveness,
Learn life's lessons and learn to trust again.

Now, the storm clouds begin to lighten,
And the sun shines through,
After the storms,
The rainbow is in full view!
God is with us and all is well!

— author unknown-

CHAPTER FIFTEEN

Gifts

He heals the brokenhearted
and binds up their wounds.
He determines the number of the stars;
He calls them each by name.
Great is our Lord, and mighty in power;
His understanding has no limit.

— Psalm 147:3-5

Of all the gifts God has given to me, the greatest came when I became a mother. Even with the challenges, being a mother and caring for my children was one of my greatest joys. To watch our children grow into productive and good citizens that are making a difference in the world is a proud moment. To watch them raise their own children is an even deeper joy!

I was a wife, mom, social worker, and then a pastor/ chaplain. It all involved a lot of love and caregiving. I did mission work in India helping an organization develop schools and orphanages, churches and pastors' training. The list could go on, but you get the gist — I never took time for myself or gave much self-love. So, cancer became my teacher in learning the art of self-love of which I am still a student. This self-love is teaching me that it is okay to take time to let yourself be nurtured and loved. I am learning that It's okay to say what I need. In fact, I have found, if you do not learn to verbalize your needs, you will never fully experience healing.

A friend whom I had helped a lot reached out to me and reminded me that when you do not let others help you during your time of need, you are robbing them of a blessing. So, my experience has taught me to begin verbalizing my needs, and to let others help on my journey too. As you do this, you will be blessed and others will have the opportunity of blessing you! A little voice kept telling me not to be so independent. Let people help you as you have helped others. This will give them an opportunity to be creative in their act of kindness and love and to be able to both give and receive with grace. Scripture tells us to cast our cares upon Christ, because he cares for us. Christ also cares for us through other people's acts of kindness, encouragement and love.

If you are facing a serious illness, this is your season to love and be loved. This is your season of mourning and of laughter, this is your season where fear loses its grip, where hope finds you looking towards a new day and where the oil of healing reaches from one soul to another. This is your season of releasing fears that have you bound.

As a woman who has had to say goodbye to body parts, I realize the significance of this journey, to be one in which no matter who we are, or what body part we must lose either internally or externally we must learn to walk a journey, which allows one to recognize the value of that body part. Then, take time to be thankful and grateful for the time your body served you. Use whatever ritual you may find helpful to say goodbye to that body part, in order to journey on. The school of life is a great teacher if we learn to listen not only with our ears but also with grateful hearts.

I believe as we draw nearer to Christ with a grateful heart, we will see that our illness begins to diminish from our minds as we focus on our lives overflowing with blessings! The blessings of family and friends who stand by your side, the blessing of a closer relationship with the Divine, knowing that nothing can separate you from His love, a security blanket of substance. When you are afraid, cuddle up in that security blanket and feel a warm peace embrace you.

Know that God is trustworthy, and your security lies in Him, not a diagnosis. Remember the Big C of Christ is stronger than the little c of cancer. As you learn to trust the One who created you, the One who knows every cell of your being, fear begins to leave as trust muscles are developed. Developing trust muscles is a workout with a big payoff.

I believe fear is one of Satan's favorite tools to defeat and discourage. Learn to speak out loud, "I resist the evil one in Jesus's name," and he will flee from you. Resist the discourager and begin praising God for your blessings. Let Him become your song, your shield, your strength, your trust. Now, be on the lookout for the surprises God has waiting for you, whether it be healing or heaven, all is good, and God is so good!

The Rev. Dr. Tim Brown, a friend and former president of Western Theological Seminary, is an amazing man of God. Dr. Brown has had two brain surgeries for adult on-set hydrocephalus and still continues to be an active man, making a wonderful impact in the world.

In a sermon he recently preached at Pillar Church in Holland, Michigan, he delivered a message entitled: "No way… there is always a way." He said that we must climb a mountain to meet the living God and sit quietly before him. It is there that God cuts the distance between heaven and earth; it is there where we meet God.

He said, "We are third day people, because Jesus was resurrected on the third day, giving the world hope." God refuses to leave us where we are in our distress, our concerns, our troubles, our illness or diseases and offers us hope. Words of hope, filled with love for all that concerns us." I invite you to come to the God of Hope and to drink from His ever-flowing fountain of grace, mercy, hope and peace as you read the following scriptures.

Scripture Resources and Focus Thoughts: Paraphrased

1. Peter 5: 5-11, Unload all your worries on Him since He is looking after you.
2. Psalm 16 I will keep Yahweh before me always, for with Him at my right hand nothing can shake me.
3. Psalm 23 Though I pass through the valley of death, I will fear no evil.
4. Psalm 91 My God in whom I trust.
5. Isaiah 41:9-14, Do not be afraid for I am with you. Stop being anxious and watchful for I am your God.
6. Psalm 27, God is my light and my salvation, whom shall I fear?
7. Jeremiah 29:4-14, I know the plans I have for you, says the Lord, plans to prosper you, to give you hope and a future.

CHAPTER SIXTEEN

The Compassionate Spirit and Re-evaluating Lifestyles

"He himself bore our sins" in his body on the cross, so that we might die to sins and live for righteousness; "by his wounds you have been healed."

— 1 Peter 2:24

About five years ago my sister's first granddaughter who was nearly four years of age was visiting a friend's house with her mother. Her mom had put her down for a nap. When their daughter awakened, she found a gun in the room and thought it was a toy. The gun accidentally went off and killed her. It was an absolutely unbearable tragedy.

To even find explanations to such a tragedy is impossible. How does a family go on after such a tragedy? Is there ever closure? My nephew and his wife were both in the Navy and I witnessed the Naval community coming together to comfort and support them in beautiful ways as God moved among them during the memorial service. Since then, God has brought new joy into my nephew's life with additional children, yet the memories of their daughter remain alive, as they should. Sometimes, the more we question why, the harder it is. Our only comfort through this tragedy came with the knowledge that our nearly four-year-old darling was now safe in the arms of Jesus.

Recently, a wonderful friend of ours with whom we have done a lot with in ministry, lost their son Dr. Joel DeVries. Joel had MS and had spent considerable time in the hospital. He was approaching his 50th birthday and had an 11-year-old son and a wife at the time of his death.

Joel was at the height of his career in atomic physics when the crippling disease of MS began to ravage his body, until it took over his brain and bodily functions. His family and friends prayed and prayed for Joel's health to be renewed. They prayed for a new medication to heal him and in the end, God healed him in Heaven.

When the news came to our friends Lee and Jean, of course they were devastated and struggled even for sleep. God, in His goodness, wrapped His love around them as He whispered gently to Jean, he is safe now, I have Him in the palm of my hand. With that assurance they could face the days ahead, knowing Joel was with God. In their pain, in the mist of tears they could say that God is good. In their pain, they could give Joel to God, knowing He saw the bigger picture for Joel's life. They believed God knew things they did not know. They knew God loved their son, and allowed grace and pain to meet each other, as they released Joel into the loving arms of God. Knowing they needed support, a group of their wonderful friends gathered with them in an intimate setting of their friends living room. Together, we remembered stories of Joel, we read various healing scriptures, and had spontaneous heartfelt prayers for them. Then we just sat quietly, holding hands, until the Spirit moved in Jean and she began singing a song of praise and we all joined in. This was a compassionate and healing night for our friends which helped them to move on.

This Christ-like compassionate spirit opens our eyes to see and feel the suffering of other people in pain. As we allow our compassionate spirit to become activated, the sufferings in the world around us becomes more pronounced and our problems less diminished. Then as we pray, our prayers become compassionate healing prayers and often in the midst of this we find areas of our own life healed. So, as you sit waiting for your chemo treatment, look around at the many faces, offer a smile, give a word of encouragement and you will see yourself as not only a cancer patient, but a patient on a journey with others who suffer. Pain suffered alone feels very different from pain suffered alongside another. Even if the pain stays, there is a great difference when another person shares it with us. You can be that balm of Gilead to others as you listen to their stories with a compassionate and prayerful heart. Then you will be ready for whatever journey you must take.

I remember two separate Christmas Eves, one from my first breast cancer surgery and the next from my second breast cancer surgery. The first time I was feeling a bit lonely and neighbors came over Christmas caroling and which brightened my spirit. After my second bout with breast cancer again another Christmas season, the Sandusky family came over Christmas caroling. They came in and read the Christmas story. We sang carols and enjoyed some Christmas treats together. It was a memorable moment as we shared our love with each other and it made a lonely day brighter thanks to their positive energy! They are a special family to me.

I remember a dear cancer friend, Sally, who even in her 4th stage of cancer was a beaming light of compassion to other patients. She often would hold the hand of another patient, listen to their journey, encourage and lift them up even in her final days of life. Sally knew what the end would look like, because she walked through cancer with her brother only a year earlier. I never saw bitterness engulf her spirit, but only love. She won her victory and now lives pain-free in the presence of the Holy One, with her brother. Let us all be like Sally, compassionate encouragers even in our pain and we can help make the day a bit lighter and brighter for the suffering, and as we do, we will feel lighter too.

My neighbors the Johnsons were wonderful examples of walking the cancer journey with God. Mary J. battled cancer for several years with a positive attitude, leaning on the Lord in the midst of knowing pancreatic cancer would take her at the age of 57. Her husband, Weldin, remarried the following year to another lovely lady, Jane. About 20 years after Mary's death, Weldin was also diagnosed with incurable cancer. Both he and his wife Jane relied on their faith and rarely complained but trusted God until his death. Even in his last days they would say, through it all, "God is good!"

Through my pastoral ministries I have found that people with faith usually have a greater resilience and are usually more positive about their diagnosis. That does not mean that they have not questioned the reason for their cancer or their loss; it does not mean they did not fight depression or fears, but it does show that when times were tough, they found a way to lean on the everlasting arms of God, knowing He would carry them through their disease or onto a new life, where they would be with their Savior forever. For them the reality of heaven became only a blink away!

My own physician's Dr. Karen and her husband Dr. Russ have been through many health challenges with their family. Dr. Karen has faced very tough challenges due to her cancer. Yet she perseveres, and believes in the power of prayer and the latest medical opportunities to help her. Through all of their challenges they remain positive and use what they have learned in medicine and their own personal challenges as ways to help others in their crisis. They are amazing examples of God's love, compassion, and grace in their healing professions. In addition, their daughter Dr. Ariel completed Michigan State Medical School and is at Oxford Seminary, teaching and pursuing a doctorate in ethics, ministry and palliative care. Ariel is a dynamic woman with many talents who chooses to make her life count for God.

About five years ago, she was flying to England and had a massive brain bleed on the airplane. She nearly lost her life and for several years had major complications. Her faith is a testimony to God's faithfulness! I am so grateful they are part of my life. They indeed are wounded healers with a heart for people and serving God.

Remember, we can either learn to handle our struggles whatever they may be, or they will surely handle us! The school of life is a great teacher if we learn to listen, not only with our minds, but also with our hearts. It is helpful to remember that our diseases are not meant to destroy us, but to teach us lessons and to awaken us to life. If we allow our pain to awaken us, we are then miles ahead on our journey and able to bless others on their journey.

CHAPTER SEVENTEEN

The Role of Music, Art and Poetry in Healing

When in affliction's valley, I trod the road of care
My Savior helps me carry; the cross so heavy to bear
Though all around me is darkness and earthly joys have flown
My Savior whispers His promise, never to leave me alone!
Chorus: No never alone, not never alone, He promised never to leave me, never to leave me alone!

— "Never Alone" (Christian hymn) Author, Anonymous
Ludie Day Pickett 1897 Public Domain

I HAVE FOUND, AS LIFE BECOMES INTENTION ORIENTATED, WITH DAILY meditation, prayer, self-care and love, that the Master Himself will direct and orchestrate our lives into a beautiful symphony where even in the midst of storms, there is peace reminding us that all is well.

There is a song in the Christian tradition that I love to sing. It is called "It Is Well with My Soul" by Horatio Spafford. Horatio was a wealthy attorney and investor. He and his wife had lost a son, and lost their business, so to help ease their pain Horatio sent his wife and four daughters on a ship to England where all four of his daughters lost their lives at sea.

In the depths of his sorrow, he penned the words to the song we know so well, "It is Well with my Soul."

The lyrics to the song say,

When peace like a river attendeth my way,
when sorrows like sea billows roll,
whatever my lot, Thou hast taught me to say,
It is well, it is well with my soul!
Horratio Spafford 1873 Public domain (Hope Publishing)

A powerful affirmation! As we face our struggles, know that all of our pain is an outreach from heaven to teach us what we still must learn so that we can become wounded healers. You may wonder if pain and suffering is God's will? Scripture tells us that God wants us to live in health and prosperity. Isaiah 53 tells us that He was wounded for our transgressions, He was bruised for our iniquities and by His stripes we are healed.

But we live in a sinful world that has contributed to environmental issues that sometimes affect our ill health. We live in a world where hatred, bad attitudes, bitterness and unforgiveness contribute to our struggles and diseases. Therefore, I believe we need to look at our lives and search our hearts to see if there is unforgiveness, bad attitudes or wrong doings within us. Then we must focus on ways to heal these areas of our lives. I would suggest praying over the issues that may arise. Ask God to help you correct and heal any wrongs that may come to light and need to be resolved. Know that God is with you when you come to Him with your concerns. As we seek to remove the burdens we carry, we should seek to have a clean heart as we open our lives to receive healing.

Another hymn that rings true in my spirit is "Moment by Moment." (1893) by DW Whittle, published by Wholesome Words.

The second, third and fourth verses are so encouraging to me.

- Verse 2: Never a trial that He is not there, never a burden that He does not bear; Never a sorrow that He does not share, Moment by moment, I'm under His care.
- Verse 3: Never a heartache and never a groan, never a teardrop and never a moan, never a danger but there on the throne, Moment by moment, He thinks of His own.

- Verse 4: Never a weakness that He does not feel, never a sickness that He cannot heal, Moment by moment in woe or in weal Jesus, My Savior, abides with me still.
- Chorus: Moment by moment I'm kept in His love, Moment by moment I've life from above, looking to Jesus till glory doth shine, Moment by moment, O Lord, I am Thine!
  DW Whittle 1893 public domain (Wholesome Words.Org)
  These words have rung true to me, and I pray for you too!

While I was going through treatments, I would meet regularly with the hospital music therapist and art therapy classes. These outreach programs were a way to put my thoughts on paper. The following is a song I wrote while in those classes. I had the privilege of presenting it at the Lemmen Holton Cancer Event in Grand Rapids, Michigan. I had a trio of singers singing the chorus, while I did the readings of each verse. The pianist quietly played the tune to "It is Well," while I narrated.

You've already read the first verses early on in this book on page 16. Here is the entire song.

JOYCE'S SONG ALL WILL BE WELL

(to the tune of It is well with my soul)
by Joyce Van Dyk

Chorus:
All will be well, all will be well.
All will be well, don't worry.
Take courage, be strong,
All will be well.

Verse 1
I remember the day so clearly,
The golden sun falling on the lake, sparkling like diamonds.
I felt an overwhelming peace as a soft inner voice whispered,
Your cancer results are positive, but be strong. "All will be well."

All will be well, all will be well,
All will be well, don't you worry.
Take courage, be strong,
All will be well.

Verse 2
At times, depression and all the decisions overwhelm me,
As I deal with these feelings of
losing my breasts, my female identity, the surgeries,
the reconstruction, the pain, the chemo, the radiation,
and the days and months and years ahead made my head swirl.
Then I recall the cross of suffering,
remembering that the big "C" in Christ is stronger
than the little "c" of cancer. And I know,

All will be well, all will be well,
All will be well, don't you worry.
Take courage, be strong,
All will be well.

Verse 3
How do you find some kind of closure?
To losing a part of your body that has served you well?
How do you find alternative ways to keep your attitude in check,
so that the days ahead are filled with healing grace and peace?
I knew my attitude would be the painting, which would color my world, and knew I wanted to include my friends in painting the canvas of this journey I was taking.

All will be well, all will be well.
All will be well, don't you worry.
Take courage, be strong,
All will be well.

Verse 4
And all was well.
Through this experience of breast cancer, not once, but twice,
I have found myself agreeing that in life,
We are not human beings, having a spiritual experience.
We are spiritual beings having a human experience.

Chorus refrain:
All will be well, all will be well.
All will be well, don't you worry.
Take courage, be strong
All will be well.

Verse 5
As we face difficult times, take heart in knowing we are not alone in our experience.
We are human beings, we are survivors, and we embody hope.
With a grateful heart, I was able to overcome these trials by welcoming the constant embrace of God and my loved ones.
Who will you invite on your journey?
Hope is important, because it can make our difficult moments easier to bear.
If we believe that tomorrow will be better, we can bear a hardship today.

Chorus refrain:
All will be well, all will be well.
All will be well, don't you worry.
Take courage, be strong,
All will be well.

Verse 6
I have learned that there is no one way to fight cancer, as there is no one way to deal with depression or grief, but if we can fight our fears with hope and be light and love, there is a future.
"For I know the plans I have for you, declares the Lord, plans to prosper you and not harm you, to give you a hope and a future."
So with encouragement, I urge myself and you to be strong, be courageous, do not be afraid, and to know whatever comes,
All will be well.

Chorus:
All will be well, all will be well, for it is well, it is well with my soul!

CHAPTER EIGHTEEN

Wrestling with Spiritual Questions

God murmurs to us in our joys, addresses us in our hearts,
but speaks loudly to us with a megaphone in our pain.
(paraphrased) C. S. Lewis, The problem of pain.

I HAVE EXPERIENCED THE TRUTH OF WHAT LEWIS SAID IN TWO distinct different ways. First, sometimes God shouts to us in our pain, to change our ways. Perhaps we need to change the way we live, how we eat, how we think, and examine how much we have let anger, unforgiveness and malice slip into our lives. If we harbor anger, unforgiveness or malice it is best to deal with these areas before it eats us up or we become sick. So make changes, and let go of that anger or whatever is eating you up and you will be healthier and happier. Secondly, in our times of suffering and pain it is often difficult to see beyond what we are facing.

That is when God shouts, I've got this! I've got you! I am your lifeline! I know you feel like you're drowning, but you're not! Just hold on, I've got you! I am your life line! Trust me! It is when we are able to trust and hold on to the lifeline, that peace begins to flow. And as peace flows, so too, patience, faith and hope grow. It is then that we begin to see how God can turn our ashes into joy.

Nevertheless, throughout our lives we all reach points where we find ourselves wrestling with spiritual questions. A friend of mine was involved in a tragic accident in which a drunk man T-boned his car. His wife was instantly killed and he was hospitalized for several weeks. It was devastating! The questions of how could a good God let some crazy drunk driver kill my wife and let the drunk man live, went through his mind like a waterfall. It took some honest questions and time before he could reconcile the pain he was feeling. Because his faith led him to believe in a loving God, whenever his heart began to long for his wife, he chose to fill his heart with sweet memories of their life together. With each memory, he began to laugh through his tears. His healing tears began a wonderful litany of memories, with thankfulness to God for a wonderful marriage and on to eventually forgiving the man who had caused the accident. To really know God, he had to wrestle through pain, struggle with doubts and unanswered questions. In the midst of his pain, he chose to think about the goodness God had provided for so many years of their married life and he began to heal.

Another pastor friend recently lost his granddaughter and wife within a month of each other. I asked his daughter how he was doing. She responded, it is hard, but Dad does not allow his grief to consume him. He is busy going on mission trips, always wanting to help others and this helps him to move on. He is the wounded healer.

As I write my heart and prayers go out to a beautiful young woman who was a member of the church I served. She has just been diagnosed with brain cancer. I cannot imagine the fear, pain and anguish she faces. I ask, God, why her? She loves you. She has a young son and a husband who both need her and love her. Please, God, do a miracle, heal her, give her hope, give her doctors wisdom and discernment. Lord, comfort and give her peace in the midst of this nightmare. Please God, for Jenny, please.

So dear reader, I wonder if you are struggling with unimaginable challenges and questions. I can imagine the fears, pain and the anguish you face. If you are struggling, I hope that you are willing to wrestle. To really know God, you have to wrestle in and through your pain. You must struggle with your doubts and be willing to live with unanswered as well as answered questions. In all of your wrestling, as you seek God, He will meet you in your pain. No matter who you are, where you come from, what religious or ethnic background you come from, or perhaps you have no religion, God still loves you and wants to enter your pain and bring you peace. Just ask.

As you struggle, take time to read the book of Habakkuk in the Bible. The book is only three chapters long and gives deep insight into conflicted feelings of pulling away and questioning God, to embracing him and feeling the hope that God will meet you in your pain.

The longer I live, the more I seek to understand the ways of God and human nature. This seeking comes out of my own struggles with health issues, life and death experiences. I believe God is good. I believe God wants the best for us, and sometimes we get in the way of God, forging ahead on our behalf. God, I believe, honors our seeking hearts — just read the Psalms which are full of prayers or people in pain. For instance, in Psalm 6 the psalmist David, a man after God's own heart, asks the Lord to have mercy on him. David asks, 'how long do I have to be in this anguish, how long do I have to endure pain? Have mercy on me O God!"

Even Jesus questioned the will of the Father when on the cross he cried out, "My God, my God, why have you forsaken me?" (Matt 27:46). Life wasn't fair for Jesus, and for God to allow His son to suffer and die, I can't even imagine! The day Jesus was crucified was the day Jesus chose to give His life over to the Father and die on our behalf for a world filled with sin and pain as He said, not my will, but Yours be done.

That was the day he paid for our sins. That was the day, light and darkness clashed and love won out on our behalf! That was the day, when sorrow and love flowed mingled down from the cross, that was the day that darkness lifted and the resurrecting power of Christ became alive! You see, in death for the believer, there is life and hope as light penetrates our darkness!

God experienced every possible feeling of wretched pain as His son suffered on the cross on our behalf. He entered into his son's pain, as a Father and Creator. And even as He entered into the pain of His loving son, He enters our pain too. When we are honest with God about our doubts, our pain, our discouragement, and our need for him, it is in those times He meets us in the valley of our pain. It is often there our questions are answered.

Even if they are not answered, we can find peace in the valley as we sit beside the still waters, basking in His Holy presence, listening to the voice of the Divine pouring out grace on our behalf. It is in the valley that our faith is grown. It is in the valley where our trust muscles begin to emerge, as God pours love into every hungry crevice that is open to receive grace and love. It is in these difficult times that we receive grace and strength to carry on.

I remember a time after going through major surgery, thinking all was well when the following evening I developed an intense UTI. I experienced unbearable gut-wrenching pain. My body became filled with sepsis. I began to shake uncontrollably and go into shock. When they discovered the cause, I was hanging on by a thread as they began IV antibiotics around the clock.

This has happened to me many times and each time there were two things that brought me back to life: one, modern medicine given stat; and two, prayers. During that night of wretched pain, a nurse brought me a CD of calming scriptures set to music. Through the pain, this scripture music was able to calm my mind, reminding me that I was in the hands of the Great Physician. I would use these scripture verses as a prayer and between the antibiotics and prayer, slowly my body began to heal. I love how God is so involved in bringing peace in times of storms.

As a patient, a pastor and hospital chaplain, I can tell you God is alive and well, moving among patients' rooms, and surgery centers, empowering physicians with wisdom, touching patients with love and grace to get through their surgeries, chemo and radiation. God is a God of renewal and restoration. Trust me, He loves and cares for you! Healing is for you! Hope is possible in the darkness. Does God care? You betcha; He loves and cares for you and for me. As you wait upon the Lord, he will reveal even more of His plans and shower more of His love, grace and faithfulness on you. Then you will know that God is good.

Remember, when you have nowhere else to turn, when all the treatments and resources have been used up, when your life is falling apart, God is still there. When your knees are sore from praying and it feels like God is not listening, God is still there. When you feel that you are entirely used up and can't make it through another hour or another day, God is still there. When lies from the enemy continue to whisper, "Just give up," God is still there.

God loves you. God is for you. God promises to never let you down, or leave you or forsake you and he promises to be your lifeline! God in

His wisdom may not do exactly what you want or when you want it, but He is faithful and no matter what happens in your life, God is there and will use all you go through for greater good. So, trust in tomorrow, trust that your unanswered questions will be revealed in God's timing. When you only see through a glass darkly, trust in God's bigger picture. Trust that your unanswered questions can lie in the hands of God who knows the beginning to the end. Trust that whatever happens in your life, God will carry you through. Or perhaps God will use another person to comfort you.

Trust that God will send the right people to be with you when the going gets tough. More recently I had major spine surgery involving four fusions. A few days after surgery I developed another painful UTI and felt quite hopeless and sick. But in God's Divine plan, my dear friend Marty showed up in my room for comfort and prayer. What a dear friend! Then my friend, Judie came in to see me and played comforting music on her flute and that indeed was a gift! Those acts of kindness from my friends will never be forgotten and I began to feel peace, knowing that all would be well and I began to heal. You see, God knows what we need even before we ask!

"And we know that in all things God works for the good of those who love him, who have been called according to his purpose" (Romans 8:28). As I have heard said many times, suffering is an opportunity to experience deep hardships and turn them into good,

When it comes to God, we have His promises that nothing will be allowed in our lives that is not for our good or too hard for us to bear. There is so much more that can be said about our suffering world. I am only making a dent in it. I leave this chapter with the thought; if you suffer without God, why not let go, give up your control and allow Him to suffer with you? Trust Him to either deliver or heal your situation or to work good from it. Let the unconditional love of God surround you and wrap you in a blanket, until you feel the warmth of His love.

Today is a new day. Be thankful for the big and little things in your life! Look for the many ways God is showing His love to you and answering your prayers. Even in your searching and waiting, God is still active.

"Ask and it will be given to you; seek and you will find; knock and the door will be opened to you. For everyone who asks receives; the one who seeks finds; and to the one who knocks, the door will be opened" (Matt.7:7-8). How comforting!

CHAPTER NINETEEN

The Season of Love Versus Fear

Peace I leave with you; my peace I give you. I do not give to you as the world gives. Do not let your hearts be troubled and do not be afraid.

—John 14:27

WHAT HAPPENS WHEN WE ARE MOVING FORWARD AND ALL OF A SUDDEN experience a halt in what we are doing or thinking, and it creates fear. That is what happened to me, when everyone was encouraging me to write about this experience of the Bye, Bye Boobie Party. Fear set in; I was afraid of revisiting some of the painful sides of my cancer experience.

I thought, who am I to write a book? Would it ever be good enough? The chains of fear are strong, especially when walking through a cancer journey. It is also compounded when you experience so many others walking through cancer, and many like me who were walking the journey over again. Fear, at times, gripped me. While many were encouraging me to write about my experience, fear kept getting in my way.

I knew the opposite of fear is love. How was I going to let love conquer fear? Truthfully, it was not until after my second breast cancer that I felt I had the courage to think about writing this book. It has taken time, but as I write fear begins to wash away, just as my hair did during chemo. So, I keep going, knowing that with each word, whatever my fear, it will wash away. Down the drain it goes! A time to mourn, a time to heal, a time for hope, a time to laugh! Let joy reign!

As I've related previously, my second diagnosis with breast cancer happened several years after my first breast cancer. I became sick from cellulitis that went quickly to sepsis. We were hiking the National

Parks in Utah. That night while sleeping in a hotel, a bug bit my right arm. When I awoke my arm was slightly red and mildly swollen. We decided to continue on our trip driving to California to my son's house in LA. We arrived at about 4:00 p.m. and I was running a fever, shaking and felt absolutely horrible. My arm by that time was bright red and extremely swollen and I knew immediately lymphedema had set in. My son called his friend, Dr. Prudence and she said to get to Cedar Sinai Hospital immediately. There they administered intense doses of IV antibiotics for a week for sepsis and lymphedema.

Six weeks later, I was back in Grand Rapids and the infection recurred. This time when I went to emergency, they did a PET scan and found my cancer had reoccurred under the chest wall, which was quite unusual after having a full bilateral mastectomy. Again, surgery and radiation. This time however, I felt stronger and knew I could beat cancer once again. And I did!

But fear is always a factor. I find that in times of crisis often people let fear dominate their thoughts. The earth is dominated by thoughts of fear and we are conditioned by those thoughts and often forget the power of our Source. We forget that with God's love active in our life, we have the power to claim and change our lives and to let the extraordinary power of God work miracles in and through us. You see, fear ties us up and love releases us!

A few practical examples of how fear can keep us from moving forward: perhaps we find ourselves in a rough financial situation and we think: No, we can't do this or that, because we have so many medical expenses and we will never get ahead. When you let fear and negative thoughts control your life it can paralyze you from moving ahead and getting out of a rough situation. Now, while we should be frugal when times are tough, it is the perfect time to release your finances to God and trust Him to lead you into a financial miracle. Perhaps, you are fearful and feel as if you can't pursue your dreams, because you don't have enough education or faith. This is the perfect time to ask for guidance from your Source and begin finding a pathway to achieve your objectives. Or perhaps, we think we can't change the negative things in this world because it's been that way too long and you feel like one itty-bitty person can't change a thing. That is doubtful, fearful and faithless thinking! The world has always been changed by one person stepping forward and encouraging others. The world has always been changed by miracles that have changed the direction of our lives.

Sometimes, when disease hits home, we may think; this is just my lot in life or it is God's will for me to have this disease. When you let negative thoughts rule your life and you think you can't then you can't. Now, if you think you can, you might; and if you think God can, you and God are on your way to a life of spiritual triumph over whatever trial you face. To combat my fears, during cancer I placed affirmation cards on my mirror and refrigerator to encourage me day by day.

I have had some great examples close to home. I have been privileged and honored to stand back and watch my son Jeffrey, who is a life coach and spiritual teacher, rely on his Source and whatever situation he is in or whatever direction he feels he must go, everything shows up and is there when he needs it. Magic, no. Magical, yes, because he has learned to ride the waves of life with expectancy, positive affirmation, trust, and seeking his Source as his director! Jeffrey has recently released an album entitled "YOU BELONG" in which he has written the lyrics to the songs he sings. The album is powerful and comforting and I believe it would be a source of healing for you. To listen, go to any major streaming service (Spotify, Apple Music, etc.) and search for Jeffrey Van Dyk's YOU BELONG album.

When my daughter Kimberly went through divorce, I was pleased to witness her times of meditation and soul searching. Mediation has been a tool for her to learn to ride the waves of life. Through this discipline she has become a stronger person and a leader professionally in developing her community. She is an amazing woman and I am so proud of her!

I witnessed our youngest son Joshua and his wife Amanda go through rough and tough struggles, but instead of becoming angry, they used this difficult experience as a teaching tool. They experienced the power of surrender, prayer, and grace and it is a wonderful gift they received. Josh and Amanda are wonderful people whose life is a testimony to God's grace in times of uncertainty.

I believe, when a person allows themselves to become vulnerable and surrenders their will to their Higher Power and trusts that guidance, then they will be on their way to a life of spiritual triumph over whatever trial they may face. As we surrender, we allow the power of God's spirit to take over and move in our lives. By ourselves, we are powerless, but with a surrendered heart we can do all things through Christ who gives us strength, and this includes all the obstacles we face on the cancer journey.

As we learn to surrender, we also gain courage and strength to face the unknowns in our lives. Again, as we learn to listen to our inner voice and the still small voice of God, it gives us courage as we enter the unknown territories of cancer and we enter with much less fear. When we listen to divine guidance, we develop a partnership with guidance and make sound decisions for our lives. The New Testament uses the phrase "handed over" when Jesus was on the cross. He handed over His pain to His Father, saying not my will, but Thine be done as He was crucified. What incredible surrender in the midst of the most horrible pain imaginable! His surrender made it possible for Him to rise from the grave and gives us the power to live with purpose as third day people!

I love the poem Footprints in the Sand written by Mary Stevenson, because it shows us how God is with us even when we do not realize it. I am sure you have read this poem in its original text, but here is a paraphrase version you may enjoy.

A guy had a dream. In his dream, he was strolling with the Lord along the seashore. His life events flashed before him over the sky. He saw two sets of footsteps in the sand for each scenario, one his and the other the Lord's He glanced back at the footsteps in the sand as the final moment of his life played before him. He noticed that when he was at his lowest and most depressed points of life, he only was able to see one set of footsteps. He asked the Lord about this because it upset and perplexed him so much. Lord, you promised to walk by my side the entire time if I made a decision to follow you. But I noticed there are just one pair of footprints throughout my most trying periods of life. I don't know why you would leave me when I needed you the most.

The Lord replied, my beautiful child, I adore and love you and I would never abandon you. In the midst of your adversities and sorrows when you saw only one set of footsteps, that is when we were going through your suffering together and I picked you up and carried you.

Paraphrased from Footprints in the Sand Poem by Mary Stevenson 1936

When we are in crisis of any kind, our pain and suffering are shared with Christ. When we suffer and surrender our lives, we die to self, we die to our limitations, we die to what we hold dear. When we surrender into the arms of Christ, we find hope, comfort and healing of mind, body and spirit. Embracing hope is a challenge to all grief and loss encounters. Finding purpose in our loss and the courage to put one foot in front of the other, to meet the challenges of the next day not only takes a great amount of energy, but also requires a great amount of soul searching and leaning on your faith.

Sometimes walking through the healing journey requires faith in God without seeing the evidence in how God is working in your life. It is a process of holding on to God whether or not we see how He is working. My cousins, Irwin, and Marcia are prime examples of walking by faith. Irwin has dealt with cancer many times over and by medical accounts he is a miracle. They keep holding on, studying Scripture and surrendering their lives to Christ. Holding on to hope requires the active participation we have talked about: prayer, surrender, meditation and hope that our mourning will turn to dancing or joy.

Many times, when we release control, we learn the power of surrender. I pray that those who read these words would receive the gift of surrender and the power to let courage lead us on our journey. I believe, as we learn to cultivate courage with our heart and soul, then when the going gets tough, we can still be courageous, because of surrender. This is where as a cancer survivor, I had to believe that the big C of Christ is larger than the small c of cancer. This is where I relied on prayer, meditation, and God's word and I began to watch my courage flourish as I went through my journey. Remember, God is not stingy with His love, grace or miracles; it's a pity we ask for so few. When your Spiritual Source is active in your life, then perfect love casts out fear and all is well!

I recently read an enlightening meditation entitled Vulnerability: A Divine Connection by Fr. Richard Rohr on Facebook. Paraphrasing Rohr, he suggests that we live in a world where everything is decaying and losing its power. This reality is difficult to come to terms with, and we spend our lives searching for exceptions. We search for something that is eternal, unending and limitless.

According to religion, this unfathomable something for which we search is God. However, many of us imagined God to be strong and all powerful - a God immune to suffering. God reveals to us through Jesus, that even I experience suffering and am part of this world finiteness.

Jesus continues to be a revolutionary symbol after two thousand years. He taught in essence, that God is not who you think God is, turning theology on its head. Jesus' enfleshment and suffering demonstrates that God is not distant.

God is not an observer, God is not simply tolerating or instantly curing human suffering, even though he can. God is participating in suffering with us. Because God enters our suffering, we can experience hope and an enduring purpose. We occasionally feel as though our flesh is being torn off, like Job did, but we continue to live. Job 19:26

When we meet the living God, in the midst of our pain, we feel another kind of life, freedom and peace. Pain and beauty are the twin faces of God. We are drawn to the incredible beauty of the divine in nature. At the same time, our brokenness and weakness draw us out of ourselves in mysterious ways. We feel them both together.

Only being vulnerable pushes us to go beyond ourselves. Most of us are distracted from our own concerns when we witness real suffering and want to make it go away. For instance, we rush toward the suffering God in the same way we rush towards a hurting child. We long to hold pain in our arms. This is why so many saints yearned to live close to suffering, because they encountered Christ in suffering. They were rescued from their lesser, untrue self.

(Paraphrased) Fr. Richard Rohr, 2021 (Daily meditation group Vulnerability: A Divine Connection).

CHAPTER TWENTY

The Beauty of Community

The Christian community was not created by human efforts, rather, God divinely called people to it. By calling us out of Egypt or our bondage to the new land, out of the desert to green pastures, out of slavery to freedom, out of our sins to salvation, and out of captivity to liberation. God has transformed us into His people.

(paraphrased) Henri Nouwen, *Reaching Out*

I WAS RAISED IN FIRST REFORMED CHURCH IN HOLLAND MICHIGAN. The Reformed Church is a Christian Church of Protestant faith which has its roots in Calvinism. Calvinism follows the theological traditions set down by John Calvin and his followers developed in the 16th century.

Being raised in First Reformed Church, in Holland, Michigan was a blessing because the heart of the church was always about the love of God, the church family (the body of believers), and the wider community at large. It was and is a church that walks with their members through times of joy and sorrow, making a difference to all who are broken or struggling through God's love. It is a church that builds people up in their faith through the word of God and prayer. I believe this is the goal of most Christian churches.

I experienced this support and love when my brother Jim died. There was such an outpouring of love, it was unbelievable. Without the support of so many and the pastoral care at our church it would have been hard to make sense of his death or to cope in the days following.

When my mother, Pearl, was dealing with her cancer, the members of First Church were her immediate support system. During that time, the pastor would be faithful in his visits to her, and the church secretary would often call to check up on her. One day when the secretary called mom, she could tell mom was down and asked what she could pray for. Mom let out a sigh and said that Dad was laid off from work and his insurance was canceled. She had huge hospital bills that had to be paid and did not know where the money would come from.

"How much is it?" the secretary asked and responded "Pearl, I know God has this. God will provide."

Just hearing those words "God will provide" helped Mom. I do not know what channels the secretary had to go through, but within two weeks enough money was collected to pay her total hospital bill! What a gift of love that was! How God moved within the hearts of that congregation to help us was a living miracle! When mom died, her funeral filled the church and the congregation was a source of healing for our family.

At another point in time, the church was also my support system. My husband had to leave for the army two days after my mom's funeral. I was pregnant with our first child, Kimberly. The church became an encouraging support system for me until I could join my husband.

The church members were also actively involved in helping our family after I had my second baby, Jeffrey. I was hospitalized for ten days, following major birthing complications. Our baby was fine, but with major complications and surgery, it was impossible to care for a nearly three-year-old and a newborn. The church members rallied and came in to help take care of our children and provided meals and God's love. These acts of endearment, in the name of Christ, grew my faith and my love for the people of God.

This is the church where I first felt the call of God in my life. This is the church that even in times of doubt encouraged my faith. This is the church that taught me the power of a community in prayer. While our prayers were not answered in the way I had hoped—that Mom would live — at the same time, I could experience grace through my grief. Grace, grace, what more can I say. The grace of God, shown through the grace of the church, embodied us through our struggles, loss and grief.

The community of believers is the strongest when it extends love, without any attachments. Just the love of God, breathing from one to another in a time of need was and is amazing! Thank you, First Church, I will always have a deep love for you and a heart of gratitude. You have helped to turn our deep mourning into dancing in the many ways God's grace worked through you.

While the church is not perfect, I do believe most Christian churches at their heart want to share the grace of God through acts of service and blessing others. I believe in the church when it hears its divine call and is active in its outreach to the poor and marginalized, the sick and suffering.

What makes me excited and joyful is when I see a church like New Community in Grand Rapids actively involved in Community Recovery Programs, helping others out of addictions, and setting the captive free. New Community, is a dynamic teaching and praying church with a divine calling to be compassionate and walking in the footsteps of Christ. They are a church who shares in the tears and joys of their fellow believers and the greater community, building love through Christ. New Community Church is led by Pastors Lew and Mark VanderMeer, excellent teachers/preachers and men filled with love for others.

The UCC church in Holland, Michigan also answers to the call of Christ through their justice-oriented ministries. They have a real passion to reach out to those groups of people who are often ignored and have been treated unjustly. They have a very inclusive ministry to people of all races and sexual orientations to love people where they are with Christ's love.

Pillar Church in Holland, Michigan where I attend, is a place where your name is known, your story is heard, and your questions are honored. It is a compassionate group of believers called out to be a forward moving group of companions bound together by the same divine call, to do ministry through the love of God, that compels them to touch the world and be a church where all are included and treated with love and dignity. Pillar Church is a reconciling group of wonderful people, led by Pastor Dr. Jon Brown. If you happen to be in Holland, Michigan on a Sunday, check out this church. You will not be disappointed!

So, for those of you who think the church is dead... seek out these types of ministries that are alive and moving forward as people of God, the *ecclesia* from the Greek, called out from the old to the new. I look for this when seeking a church. I was taught this love and calling in my early years at First Reformed Church and continue to find these types of churches wherever I go, because I look for them. When we were in California, we found Del Rey Church in Marina Del Rey, a wonderful loving and teaching church which we enjoyed. I look for churches who have a love for God, and a compassion for the world. There are plenty of dry churches, but there are many with a mission to compassionately serve and they are the wellspring of life!

If you are a cancer patient, I would strongly suggest finding an active and compassionate church that could be your spiritual director on this journey. They will walk and pray with you. They will help to build your spirit and feed your soul. They will make a difference in the way you view your life and be an aid during your illness and difficult times.

The song "The Family of God," written by Bill and Gloria Gaither, talks about being part of the family of God. The family of God, that walks with each other through their difficult times sharing in their tears and rejoicing and celebrating with each other in good times. If you are not familiar with the song, go to Spotify and listen to the words. It will lift your spirit.

CHAPTER TWENTY-ONE

Burdens Shared

Is anyone among you in trouble? Let them pray. Is anyone happy? Let them sing songs of praise. Is anyone among you sick? Let them call the elders of the church to pray over them and anoint them with oil in the name of the Lord. And the prayer offered in faith will make the sick person well; the Lord will raise them up. If they have sinned, they will be forgiven. Therefore confess your sins to each other and pray for each other so that you may be healed. The prayer of a righteous person is powerful and effective.

— James 5:14-16

THROUGH MUCH TIME SERVING PEOPLE IN CRISIS, AND MANY OF MY own personal struggles, I have realized how inadequate we are to be the captain of our souls. I have known many brave and victorious people who have faced difficult circumstances. I have been at the bedside of those suffering painful deaths. I have reached out with the gift of presence, listening intently to their pain. I have been with parents who were coping with serious issues with their children. I have held the lifeless bodies of stillborn babies in my hand and walked through grief with the parents. I have held the hands of people who had been vigorous and full of life but were now debilitated from a horrible accident, a physical disease and Alzheimer's. I have officiated at funerals that seemed to be such untimely deaths. I have counseled those going through marital issues and sat with those awaiting prison sentences.

Through all of this, I have witnessed that those who relied on a Greater Power have more strength, and experience grace and love in the midst of pain and even death. You see, God's love is never limited to what church you belong to, what faith you are, or whether or not you go to a place of worship. God's love is for all, here and now. That love has the power to alter the crisis we face and to teach us life lessons through it. There is no problem to which the love of God, manifested in our love for each other, is not the healing balm that our soul needs now.

Being a patient, on the other side of the fence, is humbling. I often felt like a diamond in the rough, especially when it came to letting my family help me with intimate changes of dressings from my cancer surgeries. But they were ever so careful and did what they had to do, without a blink, while preserving my dignity. Thank you to my dear immediate family: My husband, Dick, my children: Kimberly, Sam, Jeffrey, Pete, Joshua, Amanda, my grandchildren, Noelani Joy, Rosabella Pearl, Kaia Grace, and Levi Summit. Also, thank you to my siblings and their families, Dave and Jannelle Geertman, Marilyn and Pat Chadderdon, Karen Geertman and Ed Mendez for all of your support. My sister, Karen, flew in from California to help me, and even she with a weak stomach was a blessing! You are all amazing and are SOOO loved! The experience of cancer opened my whole essence, as I was filled with gratitude for all the folks I cherished and helped me through this journey.

I appreciated so many friends who called, visited and showed many acts of kindness to me during my journey. Sometimes, friends do not know what to say or how to respond to a cancer patient. I would suggest just being with a person and being present to their needs is a gift! Let them know that they are safe in your presence. Do not worry about silence, just let silence be and give the gift of listening, compassion and presence. It's not easy to know the pain and feel the hurt of another. Let them know that it is ok to talk about their illness, when they are ready. Never, say I know what you are going through unless you have walked that walk. Even then, every person's walk is different. Instead, echo back to them their feelings, with words like, I understand this is a difficult time for you, and if there is anything I can do to make this journey a bit easier, I would like to help. Feel free to talk about other areas of interest too, but remember to stay focused on their needs and feelings, being careful not to let your own ego or motivation get in the way of your compassionate spirit. Sometimes a bit of humor may lighten their load as well. I find it important to remind the suffering that you are holding them in your hearts and prayers while offering them compassion and love. The compassionate spirit you are developing assures you that you are on the right track, for as we hold hurting ones in our hearts, we offer to them the cup of compassion that Jesus shares with us, as he enters our pain and sorrows.

Stay in contact with your friend through texts, notes, and phone calls but be sensitive to whether they are up to talking. Practical gifts are also welcome. Bring a meal but be sensitive to food allergies and needs, offer rides to treatments, help with household chores, or offer to take the patient to lunch if they are up to it. You can send flowers, balloons, and pick up items from the grocery store but the most lasting gift you can give is the gift of presence and a gentle touch. During my last cancer experience I was blessed to have a cleaning service come to my house every two weeks. This cleaning business dedicates every other Friday to bless cancer patients with their cleaning services free of charge. What a blessing those ladies were! It makes me want to reciprocate with a service I could do! How about You?

Kindly remember to visit people only if you are healthy because often cancer patients have compromised immune systems. During this era of Covid, flu and colds please never visit anyone unless you have had all covid immunizations and then wear an N-95 mask. Follow all hospital protocols.

CHAPTER TWENTY-TWO

The Role of our Spiritual and Physical Health

Dear friend, I pray that you may enjoy good health and that all may go well with you, even as your soul is getting along well.

— 3 John 1:2

I REMEMBER ONE FINE DAY FOLLOWING CHEMO TREATMENT I WAS walking barefoot in the grass, I stopped and just stared at a piece of grass. I bent down to touch the grass and was filled with amazement. I wondered what all was involved in creating a beautiful piece of grass. I would walk to my garden filled with beautiful flowers and the essence of a flower would speak to me like never before. I would be in awe of the variety of designs on each flower petal. The clouds had stories of their own to tell! We would take a ride and I would say to my husband, Dick, "Stop, stop! Look, look at how beautiful those flowers or clouds or trees are, oh look at those mountains!"

I was in awe over the smallest things I once took for granted! My heart and spirit were awakened and overflowed with gratitude for the beauty all around me. I would spontaneously start singing and praising God for the air we breathe, for the wind that would blow through my new hair, for the rain that renewed the earth, for the sun which warmed my skin, and always the lake and the many ways it would tell a story to me of rough waters and peaceful waves. Gratitude changed the ordinary of life into the extraordinary! The Scriptures would come alive as I read them. Things I glossed over before came to the forefront and I embraced it with my whole heart! Out of darkness came light and life! In and through God's love and creation we are recreated and are new people! I found that even among decay, God can make all things new and he does!

Paraphrasing, Joyce Rupp in her book, The Cup of Life, reminds us that our coffee mugs are containers designed to hold a drink that is rejuvenating, just as we are containers meant to hold the Divine Presence. Since God resides in me, I like to think of myself as a scaled down mini ark of the Covenant. God's presence goes with me wherever I go. I carry God into each relationship and encounter.

Rupp proposes that our understanding and our encounters of God shapes our picture of God. Where do we discover this God? Hebrew sacred writings tell us that this Divine nearness is all over, continuously moving and calling to people wherever they may be. This way when Jesus lives in our hearts, we become the house of God and we carry his nearness wherever we go.

In John 15: 4, Jesus said, make your home in me. Thus, when the Spirit lives in us, we become the home of God." Isn't that beautiful a beautiful thought!

When we invite God's presence into our lives, God makes his home in us and dwells among us. God never forces his way into our lives, but guides us with his loving and gentle spirit to become one with him. As he makes His home in us, he fills it with loving goodness and plays an active role in ministering grace and mercy to our lives. God's energy is directing our lives towards goodness and service to others. You may ask, where do I find this God? God's presence is everywhere".

(paraphrased) Rupp Joyce, The cup of Life (1997) Ave Maria Press)

As you go to the market, a sports event or a concert His presence is there. He is there, in your business dealings, on wall street, in the hospitals and operating rooms, in palaces and in the slums and prisons.

Scripture tells us that God's spirit is everywhere and in everything. Listen to the words of Psalms 139:1-18.

"You have searched me, Lord, and you know me. You know when I sit and when I rise, you perceive my thoughts from afar. You discern my going out and my lying down. You are familiar with all my ways. Before a word is on my tongue you, Lord, you know it completely. You hem me in behind and before, and you lay your hand upon me. Such knowledge is too wonderful for me to attain. Where can I go from your Spirit? Where can I flee from your presence? If I go to the heavens, you are there; if I make my bed in the depths, you are there. If I rise on the wings of the dawn, if I settle on the far side of the sea, even there your hand will guide me, your right hand will hold me fast. If I say, surely the darkness will hide me and the light will become night around me, even the darkness will not be dark to you; the night will shine like the day, for darkness is as light to you. You created my inner being; you knit me together in my mother's womb. I praise you, because I am fearfully and wonderfully made; your works are wonderful, I know that fully well. My frame was not hidden from you when I was made in a secret place, when I was woven together in the depths of the earth. Your eyes saw my unformed body; all the days ordained for me were written in your book before one of them came to be. How precious to me are your thoughts, God! How vast is the sum of them! Were I to count them, they would outnumber the grains of sand. When I awake, I am still with you."

God is everywhere and in everything and as a special blessing he chooses to make His home in us and fill us with grace and mercy.

I believe, when we recognize this, we begin to look at people differently. We become more loving, kind, patient and less judgmental towards all people when we view them as image bearers of God.

Granted, some people do not display that image well, because of the darkness in their lives. Perhaps that darkness could be alcohol, drugs, sickness, depressions or other distractions that have interfered with their lives. That is why we must be gentle, loving and understanding of where another person lives and what they are going through. Let us aim towards lending a non-judgmental ear and love people where they are. Let us become the good Samaritan who cares and treats others with compassion, gentleness, a listening ear and a loving heart.

Remember, as God's sons and daughters, we carry the presence of God with us, making it our goal to treat others and all of life with love.

For some people, this awareness of God's presence being everywhere we go, is a paradigm shift. But, think what wonderful news this is! This means that we are never alone! God's spirit is with us, always the energizing force behind all we do. So as we go in for surgery, chemo or other treatments God goes with us, imparting peace and filling our cups with gratitude and joy for the life we are given.

Author Joyce Rupp, has a daily practice which is lovely. She suggests:

> "Begin by breathing in: Faithful Love
> Breathe out: Dwelling in me.
>
> Reflection:
> Hold your empty mug in your hands
> Notice the space within the mug.
> Think of the space within yourself,
> It is filled with Divine Presence.
> Sense this loving presence permeating your entire being.
> Rest in silence and tranquility.
> Listen to God, say to you; "I am here."
>
> Read John 15:1-11
> Abide in me as I abide in you.
>
> Read: 1 Corinthians 3:1-17
> Do you not know that you are God's temple and that God's spirit dwells in you?
>
> Journal your thoughts and reflections

Prayer:
Rupp has a prayer she offers, which I have paraphrased.

> Gracious God, your nurturing love has found its way into my heart and has danced a song of joy in my innermost being. Thank you for enriching my spirit, for awakening me, watering my dry places, and protecting me in my darkest hour. Even in the dark places, your love has warmed and energized my soul and surrounded me with your love. O Divine Presence, your radiant energy warms me and surges through my being, making

> all things new. I stand in awe and gratitude of the sacred mystery of your life within me. Amen.

Exercise for the day, suggested by Joyce Rupp.

> Throughout the day or when anxiety is present, place your hand over your heart and say as a calm and thankful reminder that God resides in you and you have nothing to fear.
> (Paraphrased) Rupp Joyce, (1997) The cup of Life, Ave Maria Press)

Besides caring for ourselves spiritually, we must be conscious of what we are doing to make our bodies physically strong. We are blessed to live in a world where we can learn to correct some of the illnesses we have through a better lifestyle. Perhaps, we need to look at our diet. Does our diet include 2/3 of nutritious organic fruits and vegetables, less red meats, and more fresh-caught fish and organic chicken? Eating well means using a variety of foods that will give you the vitamins, minerals, protein, calories and fiber needed to keep your body functioning well. If you are going through treatment and cannot eat properly, contact your physician and oncology dietician and they will help you manage your dietary needs. Health experts suggest that during cancer treatments, you try to keep a healthy body weight and drink plenty of fluids.

During treatments try to exercise if you can, especially walking, because moderate exercise can help you feel less tired and anxious and it can also help with depression. Consult your doctor with questions regarding exercise. Post-treatment, try to get in the habit of some type of disciplined exercise. We are Juice Plus distributors and find that taking these whole food supplements of fruits and vegetables is an easy way to guarantee that we are getting all of the vitamins and minerals necessary for our bodies to thrive. See dickvandyk@juiceplus.com.

Here are some questions to ask yourself in regard to daily well-being:

- Am I eating a well-balanced healthy diet?
- How much sugar or alcohol am I consuming?

- What is my stress and anxiety level?
- Do I have a home life free of emotional and physical abuse?
- Am I holding any bitterness or unforgiveness towards others?
- Is my spiritual life in order?
- Do I have ways in which I can reduce my stress?
- Do I surround myself with positive friends who love and support me?

Cancer feeds on weak areas of our lives. Perhaps we should ask ourselves how we can improve in the areas where we find ourselves to be weak. I love to bake and enjoy my sweets too much and struggle to give up my diet coke. I have not been as successful as I would like to be in these areas, but I try to make a conscious effort at improving. I believe that if we embrace and work on the areas we struggle with, they will become life lessons and a gift. I try to follow the twelve helpful steps of AA which I find helpful in developing a better way to do life.

As we incorporate these practices, we can hopefully move on and become all that we were intended to be and become wounded healers. As we learn to embrace our struggles with gratitude, this becomes an attitude which allows grace and abundance to overflow and we know without a shadow of a doubt, that all is well. Today, dear reader, I bless you with a cup of blessing that overflows to all of your life. You are blessed to be a blessing!

CHAPTER TWENTY-THREE

The Art of Meditation and Mindfulness

Do not be anxious about anything, but in every situation, by prayer and petition, with thanksgiving, present your requests to God. And the peace of God, which transcends all understanding, will guard your hearts and your minds in Christ Jesus.

— Philippians 4:6-7

I FIND THAT PRACTICING MINDFULNESS IS HELPFUL ON A DAILY BASIS and even more so when life throws difficult situations your way. Mindfulness is best if you can set aside a daily time for yourself to center in, breathe and listen. Mindfulness practices can be done solo or can be experienced in a community of fellow sojourners. The beauty of sharing these practices in a community is that we often benefit from each other's stories in a non-judgmental setting. Then as we meditate together, we often find experiences that transport us toward a new level of opening our mind, body, and spirit to healing.

One of the practices that I hold dear, is the practice of meditation. For me, meditation has become a form of prayer in which one finds structured ways to hear God. Christian meditation is the process of purposefully focusing on thoughts that come from scripture, a song, or writing that is meaningful to you.

Too often when the word meditation is mentioned it is often associated with Eastern or New Age practices. The difference between Christian and Eastern meditation is that in Christian meditation it is our objective to focus on God, rather than emptying our minds. Many Eastern meditators would say that their objective is also to seek the Divine, so I can't be judgmental. I think there is room to learn from each other. In some ways, they are similar, because, with any meditation, we must quiet our minds and bodies in order to open our minds to the things God wants to relay to us.

Did you know that meditation is mentioned over 20 times in the Bible? The Bible says to be still and know that I am God. In this busy world, stillness is rarely sought the way it should be. Therefore, it is important that when we meditate, we choose a time and a place to be alone, without distractions from the world. This can be a dedicated place in your home, or in nature depending on the weather. Be sure this place is free from phones, computers, or anything that might distract you.

Find a comfortable position, but not too comfortable, and never your bed if possible. It is always best to be upright and your back in a straight position. If you are in a chair, place your feet flat on the floor and your hands upturned on your thighs in receptivity. I like to close my eyes, although you can keep them open. Begin by taking three to four deep breaths in through your nose, and out through your mouth until you feel your chest rising and falling and you are quiet and relaxed throughout your body. Become aware of any tension you may be feeling and breathe peace into those places. If your mind wanders, center back to your breath.

A good way to do this is to meditate on Scripture. For example, one verse I used during my illness was, "Create in me a clean heart O God, and renew a right spirit within me." Psalms 151:10-12. You may ask what this has to do with healing. Precisely this: often our illness is caused by unforgiveness or bitterness which becomes a roadblock in our mind for growth and peace. This roadblock begins to wear away at our spirit and body. It can wear down our mental, spiritual and physical bodies until we become ill. Unforgiveness and bitterness is a tool used to defeat us.

Therefore, when we meditate on a verse such as this, we must be quiet and ask God, who do I need to forgive... be quiet and wait. When something comes to your spirit mind, dialogue with it and ask what or who do I need to forgive and why? If your mind starts to wander and you find yourself making excuses as to why you feel the need to forgive or rationalize the situation — stop. Quiet yourself, go back to the verse, read the words again. "Create in me a clean heart O God and renew a right spirit within me," and let it speak to your heart.

The words clean heart and renew spoke to me. I would meditate on the words "clean heart" and "renew." I would ask God what needs to be clean in my heart so it can be renewed. I would seek out any unforgiving spirit in me and ask for forgiveness and cleansing. I would speak words of forgiveness and release so that God could renew a right spirit within me.

This is not a time to rationalize why you feel someone wronged you. Instead, free yourself, and the one who wounded you, of all blame for knowingly or unknowingly hurting you. Be still and listen for any thoughts that may be directed towards you. Ask for clarity and discernment. Be still. Let your heart surrender to forgiveness, healing, and a renewed or right spirit. Research shows there is a direct connection of unforgiveness and bitterness to illnesses that come upon us.

After my father died, I had to go through this process of forgiveness. I held a lot of bitterness towards the way he treated me. I felt unworthy and unloved. As I worked through this process of forgiveness, it took away all of the bitterness I had harbored and replaced it with love and understanding for my father.

This process of forgiveness gave me further insight into my dad and myself. I began to understand that from his years of service during the war and flying a fighter plane it brought about a lot of trauma and fear. He covered these fears with drinking, as many soldiers did and do. I did not realize he suffered from PTSD. Dad could be a loving and friendly church-going man, but when he drank his rage controlled him; and often I or another sibling got the brunt end of it.

To make matters worse, I had a big mouth and that would even further aggravate him. I am happy to say, in the years before he died something in him changed and he became more spiritual and spirit filled, as did I. Unfortunately, he died very suddenly, and I never had that chance to say goodbye, forgive him or tell him that I loved him. Going through meditation and asking God to create in me a clean heart and renew a right spirit within me, was the change that brought about forgiveness and set me free and allowed me to love him. I believe that somehow his spirit and my spirit connected through this healing experience, as I have never since had bitter feelings towards him, and feel love for him and from him.

It was a beautiful holy experience that set me free. You would be surprised by how much hate, bitterness, grief, or sorrow we hold. When we let go of those problem areas we begin to heal our bodies and souls. So, "Be still and know that I am God." Let go and let God.

Another avenue to explore is guided meditation, where a guide takes you through a meditation using guided imagery. In this type of meditation, you begin by quieting yourself, taking deep breaths in through your nose and out of your mouth, releasing any tensions in your body and listening to the voice of the guide. You are asked to let your mind wander to your favorite place — for me it is on the beach of Lake Michigan. You hear the water gently lapping on the shore, the sun is on your back, no one is around, and in your mind perhaps you see a gentle wise man who walks toward you. As he gets closer you can see that he is Jesus. Jesus greets you in a warm and tender way and sits beside you as you talk and tell him all that is in your heart. As you listen to his healing words you can begin to visualize every cell of your body coming into alignment, every cell being made new, and you come away refreshed and renewed.

After your meditations, it is advisable to have a notebook by your side and journal your experience as soon as possible. Your journal will be a great resource for going back and remembering your beautiful life-giving meditation experience, from a life-giving God.

A few other gems I used while going through chemo and radiation treatment were to meditate on the Lord's Prayer, Psalm 23, and the Apostles' Creed. As I meditated not only on each phrase but also each word, the meaning of the prayer or creed became very personal and powerful. My treatment time seemed to go by faster and I felt more renewed.

Try it, you won't be sorry.

CHAPTER TWENTY-FOUR

Affirmations

Come to me, all you who are weary and burdened, and I will give you rest.

— Matthew 11:28

ONE THING THAT HELPED ME THROUGHOUT MY TREATMENTS WAS TO write positive affirmations. Writing positive affirmations is a practice that helps to center my mind on the good around me. and the personal goals I want for my life. You can write your own affirmations or use the ones I have provided. You can also find affirmations on the internet. Pick no more than three affirmations and recite them during the day around five to ten times until they sink into your spirit.

I wrote the following positive affirmations in my journal and transferred them to 3 by 5 index cards, which I placed on my refrigerator and bathroom mirrors. These affirmations became helpful reminders of my intentions.

Here are some affirmations from my journal that you may find helpful.

1. I am conquering my illness daily. I am strong and designed by the creator to heal.
2. I will wake up today with a clear mind. I am at peace with all that has happened, is happening and will happen. I am resilient and strong. I am an overcomer. I will face the challenges that come with this cancer journey with the Divine by my side, giving me strength.

3. I release my past and live with serenity, knowing I am worthy of love and care.
4. I honor the divine within me and in others. I let my light shine and when darkness tries to creep in I do my best to focus on what is good, pure, right and beautiful!
5. I am blessed with an incredibly supportive family and friends. My tribe, my community stands with me in prayer and are willing to lend a helping hand or listening ear. All I need to do is to ask and they will be there.
6. God is my source for all material and spiritual needs. God provides all my needs. I trust my healing journey to God.
7. I use all of my experiences and knowledge to benefit my life and others.
8. I trust my physicians and medical team to give me exceptional care and bless them for their work.
9. I am filled with gratitude for the beauty that surrounds me in nature and for the moments of silence that gives me peace.
10. I choose to radiate love, joy and gratitude and am thankful for moments of joy and peace that comes my way. I am a radiant survivor.
11. I choose to see the divine in myself and others and send out loving vibrational energy to myself and those I surround.
12. I honor my need to rest and recharge so that I can heal and grow stronger. I eat healthy nutritious foods that flood my body with strength.
13. I am surrounded by positive people and positive energy that manifests itself through good encounters in my life.
14. All of my interactions with medical personnel will be positive and pleasant.
15. My surgery (or other treatments) will go well and my body will heal and grow strong again.
16. My discomfort or pain is temporary. I rise higher than my pain and know I am getting better daily.
17. With God's help I can do all things, that includes surgery, treatments and making decisions on this cancer journey.

18. I remain feminine regardless of what has been taken away from me. Cancer does not define me and cannot steal my innermost joy. I am a crazy, brave, strong and tenacious woman! I will beat cancer! Just, watch, wait and see!
19. I live with an attitude of gratitude and project radiance and love on my journey
20. I honor all that I am. I honor my tears and disappointment and try to seek balance in all my decisions. I release all obstacles that keep me from being grounded and healed.
21. I am thankful for this beautiful day and the possibility it holds. I have been given new eyes to see the limitless beauty that surrounds me. I start each day reflecting on the blessings and beauty that surround me. I will never take life for granted again!
22. I am focused on doing what I was put here on earth to do, to glorify God.
23. I am strong, I am an overcomer, I can beat cancer. Today I am rewriting my story as a survivor. I am moving forward executing the challenges that are before me with God as my co-pilot.
24. I am here for a reason. Nothing about my life is an accident. I was created as one of God's beautiful daughters and I will smile and shine!
25. Fear does not control me, as I replace fear with faith. Every time fear rears its ugly head, I will stare it down, I talk it down and put it in its place. I refuse fear and embrace courage. I will remember the words of scripture from Isaiah 41:10 that says "Fear not, for I am with you; Be not dismayed, for I am your God. I will strengthen you, Yes, I will help you, I will uphold you with my righteous right hand."
26. Cancer has no place in my life. I know that the big C in Christ is stronger than the little c of cancer. Hope is my light to recovery. Hope resides in my spirit and I say yes to it!
27. I release anything in my past that is hindering wellness such as bitterness, unforgiveness, and jealousy over to the Divine for healing and seek to live with calmness and serenity.
28. I have the courage to fight cancer one day at a time! I am a survivor and I will empower other cancer patients. With

faith and hope on my side miracles will happen. I expect a miracle!

29. I will emerge from this cancer journey victoriously. I know there is light at the end of the tunnel and I will get there. I believe that today's struggles are developing tomorrow's strength. I know that I can get through anything because God is with me and for me…therefore I am stronger than I think.
30. Every roadblock I face moves me forward with confidence. Even in my weakest moments an inner courage keeps me going. I will never give up until God calls me home.
31. My scars will heal and so will I. I will allow my scars to turn to stars for all to see. I will become the wounded healer for someone else on their journey.
32. I will fight to allow my dreams to come true for me and my family. I will plan my bucket list and move in the direction of accomplishing those goals!
33. Cancer may have started this fight, but I will finish it proudly, valiantly and courageous. I am a woman of essence, substance and strength. My heart strings are loving and tender and balance my tenacity with compassion and grace. As I face each day I grow stronger in mind, body and spirit.
34. I will fill my fears with faith, so that my fears are extinguished and no longer block my thought process. With the Divine living in me I can release my cares to the God who created me and will work all things towards his good purpose and plan for me.
35. My cancer cells become weak as I become strong in mind, body and spirit.
36. I visualize every abnormal cancer cell being gobbled up like pac-men as new cells regenerate and begin to heal and repair my body. I see new pathways firing in my brain to bring clarity to my mind. I am energized as all things become new!
37. I remain thankful for all the medical procedures that work to help me overcome the dis-ease. I fight, believing all will be well.
38. I am not what I have. I am who I choose to be, a woman of worth and beauty confident in my battle against this enemy. I release all tensions and worries that have bogged me down and

release thoughts that are pure and good, aligned with a higher purpose.

39. I am strong because my faith holds me through this journey. God wraps his loving arms around me, comforting and giving me peace each step of the way. I am thankful for this Divine love!
40. I listen to my inner self, knowing that the Divine that resides in me and gives me confidence, courage and conviction to carry on and fulfill my life's mission.
41. I live a life of peace and gratitude knowing that the grace and love of God is unconditional. I know that I am here to love and give love away.
42. I am a wounded healer, helping others in their struggles. I am living an abundant life free from fears filled with internal joy and peace as I melt into the goodness of God and this life for which I am so grateful!
43. My cancer or illness has not been given to me to discourage me, but rather to awaken me to all the blessings and possibilities God has for me.

I can do all things through Christ who gives me the strength to preserve and to carry on in this life and in the next. I know that all is well and that God holds the big picture in my life, so that all is well with my soul!

Good affirmations for breast cancer can be found all over the Internet. For instance, www.survivingbreastcancer.org has some lovely affirmations and meditation guides for healing. Perhaps, you want to write your own affirmations as I did. Writing your own affirmations is a way to ponder and think about what you need and want to say.

Begin each day, focusing on positive thoughts and what you are grateful for. Start a list of the things and people in your life that you are thankful for. Be optimistic. Rejoice and give thanks with a grateful heart!

I often will do deep breathing guided meditations that I find helpful. You can write your own guided meditation but let this meditation that

I wrote be a guide. Normally, I would audibly do this as a guided meditation with a person or a group of people. For the book's sake read through this mediation first and then follow the steps. If you have a friend with a calming voice perhaps, he or she could read the steps for you. It often helps to play some quiet, relaxing piano or guitar music on a CD, while someone gently guides you through the steps. Let's begin.

Meditation:

1. Begin by finding a straight comfortable chair. Get your wiggles out and then be still. Keep your feet on the floor and your hands on your lap open to receive.
2. Begin by taking three deep breaths in through your nose and exhaling out through your mouth. Imagine yourself sitting by a calm waterfront or a lovely garden. Feel the gentle breeze, the lapping of the water on the shore. Or imagine yourself in a lovely garden, smell the fragrance of the garden flowers. Notice how the garden is aglow with vibrant colors of yellows, orange, pinks, fuchsia, and blue flowers as the earth surrounds you with beauty. Inhale the lovely smells. Sense the gentleness of the day and the gift of life that calls you to itself.
3. Next, slowly take a few more deep breaths in through your nose and exhale through your mouth. Breathe in deeply and slowly exhale. As you take a deep breath feel the tension slowly release from the top of your head, to your forehead and resting between your eyes. Let the tension release around your temples, around and down to the tips of your ears. Feel the tension relax from your cheekbones to your mouth and down to your chin and neck. Know your body is thanking you for this relaxation exercise as your shoulders and neck begin to relax. Your body has been yearning for such a time as this. Feel the tension begin to melt from your shoulders down your arms to your fingertips. Just wiggle your fingers gently and feel the tension release.
4. Take another deep breath and as you exhale, feel the tension begin to fall from the base of your neck, down between your shoulder blades where much tension has been held, and down your thoracic spine to the bottom of your rib cage. Let your

spine relax, oh so much tension you have held in this area. Just let it go. Feel the warm energy transfer to your heart, your abdomen, your organs. Just relax as your body enjoys these moments. With each breath tension begins to fall from your hips down through your ribs and pelvis. Notice your tired legs are relaxing from the thighs, knees and around the muscles of your calves and out through your feet and toes.

5. Take a final deep breath. Breathe in deeply and slowly exhale. Just let the remaining tension melt away like butter. As you are relaxed, imagine you can see your cancer. What does it look like? Where is it located? What is it saying to you? Be still.

Imagine your cancer saying it no longer wants to be a part of your life. And you agree. Now visualize those cancer cells being gobbled up like pac-men and leaving your body. If you are experiencing pain, say hello to it. Tell the pain how it makes you feel and that it no longer has permission to control you. Tell your cancer and any pain that you may be experiencing that it is time to leave. Thank your cancer for the life lessons it has taught you and how it has awakened you. Tell your cancer that it now no longer serves any purpose in your life or God's plans for you. Tell your cancer that you are a child of God and that the dis-ease has no rights or power over you and it must leave; it is time to say good-bye once and for all in Jesus name.

6. Take a final deep breath in and exhale slowly, experience the warm and calming sensations going through your body, feel the tears of joy, as you thank your body and Jesus for allowing you this experience.

By developing a positive attitude, you can train your conscious and subconscious mind to draw more positivity into your life. In order to eliminate negative thoughts you must remove yourself from unwanted distractions and take time for silence. You must believe in yourself and train your conscious and unconscious mind, asking God to work with and through you. You have a right to give your conscious and unconscious mind instructions and they will deliver what you want and more. Surround yourself with people who make you smile, laugh and are encouraging. This is not to say that we can never have a bad day or go through our ups and downs; however, the intentions of a positive attitude combined with medicine and God's healing hand, will be a gift that will help you take this journey to the next level as you become the wounded healer.

CHAPTER TWENTY-FIVE

Why Does a Good God Allow Suffering?

My comfort in my suffering is this:
Your promise preserves my life.

— Psalm 119:50

WHERE ARE YOU, GOD?

Why are You so silent when I cry out to you day and night for direction, for an answer and all is silent? What are you trying to say to me in these silent times when grief fills my heart and there seems to be no answers? If You are a good God, then why is there so much suffering? Not only am I asking about the cancer patients with whom I journey, but the incredible amount of suffering worldwide.

Wars, shootings, natural disasters, destruction, hunger, all kinds of diseases. Why do young children die? Why is someone taken from us in the prime of their life, leaving a young family? It makes no sense, at least not to me! If you are a good God who loves and cares for us then why, oh why, do we have to experience the raw, unfiltered pain of suffering? Why are some prayers answered and others seemingly bypassed?

Why does a good God allow suffering is a question that has been asked forever. As both a primary and secondary sufferer, I have yet to find the answers to this question, but I had some glimpses and insights on the subject and the mystery of God.

As Christians, we believe that God loves us and desires for us to prosper and be in good health, to live a peace-filled and happy life. So, if God is sovereign, then why does He allow suffering and why doesn't

He stop suffering? The age-old question: why does God allow old people who are ready to die, to live; while a young child dies of cancer or some other dreadful cause? Why does He allow hunger, when there is an abundance of food? Then, where is God in the midst of abuse, domestic violence, human trafficking and mass shootings? Where is God in the midst of wars and genocide? Where is God in the midst of your personal struggles and your darkest hour?

These are questions that can drive a person crazy if you focus only on the whys of life. These questions will always be with us. Remember, that trust requires unanswered questions and that is okay; it is how we grow. We may never fully have the answers to life's complex questions, so we must choose to focus on what we inherently know: That God's very nature is good. And in His goodness, He is with us and walks with us in our sufferings and shares our tears. Just because something doesn't seem good or feel good, does not mean that God is not good. Remember, we only see a part of God's greater plan.

As we experience suffering, we at times have the privilege and insights to grasp a glimpse of the mysteries of God, but often we see through a glass dimly. The apostle Paul, when addressing the Corinthians says that we know only in part; we see through a glass dimly, and we will not know all things until we meet Jesus face to face in heaven, where there is no more suffering, pain, or tears (1 Corinthians 13:9-10). Until that time, we live in a space of trusting God with our unanswered questions, knowing He will reveal what must be revealed when we are ready. And when He does reveal His mysteries to us, it is in a loving way so that we can feel comfortable putting our cares and concerns in His hands.

In my personal life and as a pastor and chaplain I have experienced my own share of suffering, as well as walking alongside the suffering. I remember sitting beside parents whose young twin babies lingered between life and death, hoping desperately for a miracle or divine intervention for their children. To their heartbreak the babies passed and I was asked to officiate their funeral. I find that sometimes, God intervenes and people live. There are other times when all of the tears, prayers, agony and the best of medicine could not help and he or she passes from this world to the next.

During these times, I could vividly recall my own agony as I begged God to save my son Joshua, who was struggling between life and death for weeks in the hospital when he was eleven years of age. I knew how these parents struggled; I could feel their hurt, pain, exhaustion, their questions. My son lived, while others still struggled. Some by the grace of God were healed, others not.

When a child dies a parent always feels, why should my child die while I still live? A typical question most any parent could relate to. Then I go back to the day my brother Jim died at age 16. I remember my parents feeling that same way. I remember my mother swallowed up in raw grief, our family mourning for a son, a brother who was healthy one day and dead the next. I remember my parents saying, why Jim? Why not one of us?

Most parents feel that they would gladly give up their life for a child. That's a parent's love. When older people die, they take with them the past, but when children die, they take away the future. All the hopes, dreams and aspirations a parent has for them is gone and the loss is immense. Suddenly, life isn't going the way we had hoped or planned. In these times, it may feel as if God has betrayed you, walked away or stopped listening. Sometimes the pain is so raw that you grasp for anything that might provide relief. Sometimes you are so tired that all you do is sleep, or perhaps you cannot sleep at all, as your mind wanders in so many directions.

I have learned that the dynamics of death are different for everyone and every family. There is no one way to grieve. Each must grieve in their own way, in their own time.

I will always be grateful for our church family and friends whose prayers held us up and were a real source of strength and healing for us during my mother's illness and passing. I fondly remember the woman my mom worked with at Holland High School. Eddie H. was one of the kindest ladies I have ever known. She was like a sister to my mom through the death of my brother and mom's illness. She continually checked on our family to make sure we were okay. She had such a kind, tender, compassionate heart and I will forever be grateful for her love as well as the love of First Reformed Church and our community.

Losing my brother Jim was the beginning of a series of hellos and goodbyes, of gains and losses and how they impact life. Healing takes time. No one grieves the same, yet there are universal themes we all share. The raw hurt, the disbelief that this painful experience is upon us and the loss of our identity. The grieving one may ask, who am I now that my loved one is gone? The physical, emotional and spiritual symptoms of grief is a process. Grief has no rules, it takes whatever time it must and it changes our lives forever. I did not know how hard it would be to say goodbye to my brother, mother and dad, but I knew it would be harder if I did not say it: "Goodbye, my dear loved ones.

Where is God in the midst of sickness and death??? Sometimes, we do not see Him, but from personal experience I can tell you He is there. During your deepest pain, God's presence is there, grieving your deepest cries. He is there wrapping his arms around you, comforting you, carrying you and sharing in your hardest moments of life. He is there, providing peace and grace and hope to see you through.

My hope is this, that my brother, mom and dad no longer live in the place where they were laid to rest. They now live with Christ and that I shall see them again. This hope transcends the pain we feel. As I mentioned before, when that dove flew away from the gravesite into the heavens, I knew there was hope, yes hope, in the midst of pain. I looked around at the friends and family gathered at the gravesite and felt an overwhelming amount of thanks for the people who wept with us in our pain.

Each time I gather with families who are in grief, I thank God for those who stand with us in the sacred place to pray and comfort the mourning. You see, God is there in tangible and intangible ways even when we cannot see Him. Sometimes it feels like our grief and the weight of our sorrow crushes us into the ground and that grief sometimes feels endless. One day can be good, while another just a trigger of something can spark grief again. Grief comes like waves upon the seashore, one minute the waves are calm and the next waves can pull you under in a storm. But grieve we must. Each to grieve in our own way, our own time.

But the good news is that grief and mourning are not the end. Life is the end. It is the end of a new beginning. God speaks joyfully of the season that follows grief when he announces that joy comes in the morning. God speaks of a new day coming when we will enter Zion, singing with everlasting joy, a day when sorrow will be no more, when our tears will be wiped away, when our mourning shall be turned to joy, an everlasting joy! (Revelation 21:4). This is my hope, our great reunion in heaven, reunited again with loved ones and being ushered into the presence of the Lord whose light shines brighter than the sun!

I don't believe God keeps us in total darkness concerning the whys of life and our struggles, but there are many mysteries in the wisdom of God that are unanswerable until we reach heaven. So, until then, we trust and rest in the infinite wisdom of God and His goodness and the hope we have in the Resurrection.

CHAPTER TWENTY-SIX

The Strength of Testimonies

... and the people all tried to touch him, because power was coming from him and healing them all.

— Luke 6:19

I WANT TO SHARE A FEW MORE LIFE STORIES FOR YOUR ENCOURAGEMENT. The names have been changed for privacy and as you read these stories, realize that your journey may be different, so follow your own heart and the advice of your physicians for your life. These stories are for your encouragement only.

Grace, a young mother of two, like me had spent many summers at the beach soaking up sun. She was in her thirties when she noticed an odd shaped mole on her shoulder that bothered her. She saw a dermatologist and the results came back as stage-four malignant melanoma. After two surgeries and a year of chemo she is now six years cancer free. Grace says, "Every day I look back and praise the Lord for healing me. My scars remind me of that painful time, but I choose to embrace what God has done for me, because I would not be who I am today, without the disease of cancer. I choose to allow my scars to become the stars that remind me of God's goodness."

LuAnne, a 60-year-old woman with a fireworks spirit, began to experience a great deal of unusual bleeding. She went to see her gynecologist and they discovered a cyst on her left ovary. She was diagnosed with ovarian cancer. She had a hysterectomy followed by months of chemotherapy. She had regular scans and it appeared as if she was doing better. Seven years later the cancer reared its ugly head as another tumor was found, requiring surgery followed by six months of chemo and scans repeated every six months. Three years later cancer reappeared and LuAnne enrolled in some new clinical trials that offered hope.

LuAnne, is now in remission and lives life to her fullest with her feisty spirit. She would be the first to say that God is so good! She will be the first one to come over to pray and encourage those going through similar experiences. She indeed embodies the spirit of the wounded healer. In her spare time Luanne enjoys the outdoors and finds nature to be her healing space. Most of all she enjoys her family to the fullest.

Pam, is an active woman in her 50's. Her first reaction to finding out she had breast cancer was shocking. She said, I knew something was not right. Treatments followed so quickly after my diagnosis that I barely had time to think. My husband and children shared some of my first tears and immediately got on board. They were my strength throughout the cancer journey and crucial in my recovery. If I had to point to anything in my recovery process it was staying positive. Prayer, meditation, deep breathing and visualizing my body becoming whole helped me through the long days. I would listen to sounds of nature on CD's, go for walks in the woods and just breathe in the goodness of creation. I would try to hug a tree, smell the flowers and just experience these moments to the fullest. My spirituality grew and it made me realize how blessed I am. Blessed to have been given the time to embrace those I love and to move forward with faith in my God and faith in all the medical procedures provided for me.

Bonnie, is a two-time cancer survivor. She was first diagnosed at age 42, then ten years later at 52. After being cancer free for ten years she was religious about getting her mammograms and checkups. She had an appointment for a mammogram and when she arrived at the clinic, they had an emergency and were running late. The scheduler asked if she would like to reschedule? Bonnie had this gut feeling just to wait and stay, rather than to reschedule. Bonnie was able to get the mammogram later in the day, and it showed a small area that was questionable. A biopsy was scheduled and they discovered invasive ductal carcinoma in situ. She had surgery and radiation therapy and recovered from that journey. Her advice is to always follow your heart or gut feelings when it comes to cancer. If she had left the mammogram appointment and rescheduled, it may have been too late in discovering her tumor. Bonnie had a positive attitude, knowing she had beat cancer once, she said I can do it again. Her advice to others is to follow your inner instincts, learn as much as you can about your cancer, eat well, exercise, stay positive, do self-talks and keep the faith.

According to the Susan Komen Cancer foundation the median age of diagnosis of breast cancer in the United States is 63. The median is the middle value of a group of numbers, so about half of women with breast cancer are diagnosed before the age of 63 and about half are diagnosed after the age of 63. The median age of diagnosis varies by race and ethnicity.

Kathy, received the news of her cancer shortly before Christmas and remembers sitting around the twinkling lights of the Christmas tree with her family wondering if this would be her last Christmas. But as she sat there with her loved ones, she began smiling, laughing and making light jokes with them. Her daughter began singing, O you better watch out, you better not cry cause Santa Claus is coming to town. They gave me gifts to open. The first gift I opened had a big red bow with a card that said HOPE. The card said, mom you have hope, because you will have all of the best doctors and good medicine working for you. You have hope because God is for you and your family stands with you. You have hope, because you have survived so much in the past and you will survive this cancer diagnosis too! As I sat with my family amidst the glow of twinkling lights I knew then, cancer was not my death sentence and that I had hope for a future. As the days went on, I felt this inner strength growing stronger and my positive attitude towards survivorship put my mind in the right place to influence every cell in my body towards that goal. She would be the first to tell you that where there is life, there is hope. There will be days when life is overwhelming and pain, drugs and chemo brain bogs everything down, but do not give up! Live each day as the gift it truly is. Rest in God and let Him carry your burdens.

Rachel, was at a women's conference, and walked by a mobile mammogram bus and peeked in. A technologist asked if she could help her. She said, I'm just curious. I am up to date with my mammogram, but I have a few questions for a friend who is financially strapped and can't afford a mammogram. The technologist gave Rachel a card and told her to have her friend give her a call. She said, we never turn anyone away if they want a mammogram. There are programs for financial services for those who are unable to pay and we can get her in touch with them.

Rachel gave the information to her friend who set up an appointment and was diagnosed with early-stage breast cancer. She had a lumpectomy and found the resources she needed to provide the care she needed. Rachel's advice is that when an opportunity presents itself, try to take it because it may not present itself again, and who knows, you may be helping a friend too.

Mary, a retired physical therapist, was loyal in receiving her annual mammograms but this time a lump was discovered. A biopsy revealed she had invasive breast cancer. Mary began to imagine the worst until she met with her care team. Prior to meeting with Mary, her care team met as a tumor board to discuss Mary's case and to map out the best course of treatment for her. They explained to Mary her best options, which gave her a great amount of relief. They also recorded the meeting so that Mary could review it again at home. Her oncologist offered the option of a lumpectomy just the removal of cancer, followed up with radiation and hormone therapy, which she chose. Mary was so thankful for all of the positive care she received and has bounced back. She now enjoys her retirement, and family more than ever. Mary says, "I don't have time to waste, I will enjoy life to the fullest, with my faith in God as I journey on."

Ann's life was suddenly turned upside down with the unexpected divorce from her husband, who left her with three children to raise. She was an active woman who owned her own business. She was also active in her children's activities and her church. Six months following her divorce, she was diagnosed with stage 4 breast cancer. You would think that she would have just crumbled with such news, but not Ann. She knew she had to be strong for her children and she bolstered herself up with pep-talks. Ann, being a spiritual woman, began to put faith notes throughout her house, trusting in a God of love and healing. She memorized scripture after scripture on healing and God's provision, until those verses were locked in her heart and mind. She read positive affirmations daily and all of this gave her the courage and peace which helped her to fight the cancer and to win the battle.

Ann had a double mastectomy and lymph node removal and was put on various cancer fighting drugs. The battle was tough, but Ann said each day, my help comes from the Lord, who made the heavens and the earth and who can heal me."

With a large extended family and dedicated church friends who helped and encouraged her, day by day, she began to improve. Ann said she knew deep down in her soul that she would be okay. She knew that it would be a rough ride but she believed she would be able to see her children grow and marry someday. Ann would go on to say, with everything I have been through, God was with me. These experiences with life and death have changed the way I see things; it has given me clarity into the fragility of life. Every day I see blessings that I did not see before and my love for God, my family, and friends has become my biggest gift." Amen, I say to Ann, you go girl! God is with you! Through all of her trials, Ann certainly is a witness of someone who has turned their scars to stars and is an inspiration to all who meet her.

These stories all encompass a spiritual direction to them, because I have witnessed through the years how difficult it is to go on any cancer journey or other tragedy without divine help and guidance. If you are in the hospital, feel free to contact your hospital chaplain for guidance. If you are at home, feel free to contact a pastor, a spiritual director or a counselor who can help guide you on your journey.

Most of all, feel free to lift up your concerns to the Lord, your Creator who loves you and desires that you live well.

CHAPTER TWENTY-SEVEN

The Divine Dance

I love Henri Nouwen's book Turn My Mourning Into Dancing. Paraphrasing Nouwen, he suggests that mourning makes us feel impoverished. It makes us realize how small we are. The Divine Dancer calls us to stand up and take our first steps in the midst of our suffering. Jesus enters our grief, our pain and sorrow, takes us by the hand and gently raises us to our feet, and extends an invitation to dance, because he suffers alongside us, not in addition to it. We discover a method to pray in the same way as the psalmist. "For you have turned my mourning into dancing. Psalm 30:11, Because God's grace is found in the heart of our sorrows.

As we dance, we come to the realization that we don't have to remain in the tiny area of our sorrows, God's grace is found into the bigger dance with us and the Divine One. And we discover that we are richer when we are present with God and God's people. We learn that the entire planet serves as our dance floor. God has invited other people to dance, making our steps lighter as a result!

(Paraphrased) Henri Nouwen, *Turn My Mourning into Dancing, page 13. Word Publishing Group a division of Thomas Nelson Inc.*

I HAVE LEARNED THAT PAIN SUFFERED ALONE IS VERY DIFFERENT FROM pain suffered alongside another. This pain of suffering together with compassion, opens us up one to another so that we can share in others tears, meet each other's needs, and dance with the Divine Dancer as we are encouraged to take our first steps towards turning our mourning into dancing!

It is with an attitude of gratitude to our gracious God from whom all blessings flow, that I write these words: Friends, be blessed to:

Go forth with renewed life and hope.

Go forth with thanksgiving and gratitude for all that surrounds you!

Go forth renewing your faith and hope in God, who is able to do exceedingly above all you can ask or think, as the Divine walks with you on this journey.

Go forth with a compassionate heart to touch others on their journey. Go forth, with renewed faith in the wonderful mystery of God becoming flesh to live among us inviting us to be the wounded healers as we give and receive!

Go forth and be blessed to be a blessing!

CHAPTER TWENTY-EIGHT

An Additional Resource: A Public Resource For Healing

THE FOLLOWING IS FROM MY MODIFIED, PARAPHRASED PUBLIC SERVICE for healing: from *The Book of Common Prayer.*

> L. O God of peace, you have shown us that salvation comes by returning to you. Our strength and peace will come from a quiet and peaceful spirit which you instill in us as we rest in your presence. By the power of your spirit lift us to your presence so that we can be still and know that you are God.

Scripture:
Assign readers to Isaiah 53 1-5
James 5:13-16
Matthew 5:24-34

Silent Reflection (on scripture and holding in your heart those who need healing.

Prayers of the People

L (Leader). Let us pray for those who are suffering.

Gracious God, we are aware that you want to give us life and deliver us from our infirmities. Please bring health and healing to those who are ill in body, mind or spirit. Grant wisdom, compassion and patience to all medical professionals. Give the dying peace, and by your grace support the bereaved. Bring everything that is damaged in our lives, our county and the globe back to wholeness and peace, so that we may experience peace and heaven on earth in all its glory. Amen

Litany:

L. You are the God who does wonders, and with you is the well of life.
P. Hear us Oh God.
L. God, your will is for health and salvation.
P. Heal us Oh God.
L. God, grant your healing grace to all who are sick in mind, body or spirit, so that they may be whole.
P. Hear us God of Life and make us whole.

Let us Pray:

L. God, we confess our faults before you and beg your pardon. May we mature to the point when, like Jesus, we no longer want exact revenge, but rather live lives characterized by forgiveness, peace, love and the fruits of the spirit. God, please break the cycle of evil that keeps us enslaved rejecting your love. Open your arms and have mercy on us loving God and by your gentle spirit heal us. Amen.

LORD'S PRAYER (Unison)

Our Father who art in heaven, hallowed be thy name, thy kingdom come, thy will be done on earth as it is in heaven. Give us this day, our daily bread and forgive us our sins as we forgive those who sin against us. Lead us not into temptation, and deliver us from evil for thine is the kingdom, and the power and the glory forever. Amen

L. May God the Father bless you. God the Son, heal you, God the Holy Spirit give you comfort, strength and peace. In the name of the Father, Son and Holy Spirit, Amen.

People who desire healing can now come forth for anointing of oil, laying on of hands and prayer from the prayer team or pastor.

Go in peace dear readers and be blessed to love and become wounded healers. All will be well!

References/Bibliography

Special Sections: Questions for your health care provider by Spectrum Health Hospital (now, Corewell Health). informational cancer pamphlets.

Ramsey, Noorbergen, (1981) *Living with Loss.* William Morrow Press

Rienstra Marchiene, (2003) *Swallows Nest.* William and Eerdmans Publishing Press

Lewis Jacqui (July 9, 2002) *Sermon Good Grief,* July9 @middlechurch

Lewis CS (1961) 3rd edition, *A grief observed.* Seabury Press

Lewis CS (1940) *The problem of pain.* Simon and Schuster press

Author Unknown*: Hymn Never Alone.* (1897) Ludie Day Pickett Press, Public Domain

Spafford Horatio (1873) Hymn, *It is Well.* Hope Publishing, Public domain

Whittle DW (1800's) Hymn, *Moment by moment.* Wholesome words publishing

Irving Washington, (1945) *A sacredness in tears.* Quotable Quotes by Good Reader Internet

Kessler David (2020) *The six stages of grief.* Simon and Schuster, Scribner Imprint

Stevenson Mary (1936) *Footprints in the sand.* Antioch Publishing

Rohr Richard, (2021) Daily Meditation Facebook Group. Vulnerability *a Divine Connection.*

Nouwen Henri, (1995) *Reaching Out.* Doubleday publishing Press

Nouwen Henri (2004) *Turn my mourning into dancing.* Word publishing/ of Thomas Nelson, Inc

Gaither Bill and Gloria, (1970) Hymn *The family of God.* The Celebration Hymnal

Rupp Joyce, (1997) *The Cup of Life.* Ave Maria Press

The Book of Common Prayer (1662 revised 1979) The Episcopal Church

Printed in the United States
by Baker & Taylor Publisher Services